They're Not Stupid

Rob,
I truly appreciate
all you've done for
youth.
Joe

They're Not Stupid

Unleashing the Genius of Each Student

Joseph DiMartino and Jason B. Midwood

ROWMAN & LITTLEFIELD
Lanham • Boulder • New York • London
and
The Center for Secondary School Redesign

Published by Rowman & Littlefield
A wholly owned subsidiary of The Rowman & Littlefield Publishing Group, Inc.
4501 Forbes Boulevard, Suite 200, Lanham, Maryland 20706
www.rowman.com

Unit A, Whitacre Mews, 26-34 Stannary Street, London SE11 4AB

In Cooperation with the Center for Secondary School Redesign

British Library Cataloguing in Publication Information Available

Library of Congress Cataloging-in-Publication Data Available

ISBN 978-1-4758-3044-6 (cloth : alk. paper)
ISBN 978-1-4758-3045-3 (pbk : alk. paper)
ISBN 978-1-4758-3046-0 (electronic)

∞ ™ The paper used in this publication meets the minimum requirements of American National Standard for Information Sciences Permanence of Paper for Printed Library Materials, ANSI/NISO Z39.48-1992.

Printed in the United States of America

Unless otherwise specified, figures are courtesy of the Center for Secondary School Redesign.

Contents

Foreword   vii

Preface   xi
    Joseph DiMartino

Acknowledgments   xiii

1   The Ecosystem of Student-Driven Learning   1
2   Culture of Inquiry   13
3   The Power of Network   29
4   Shared Leadership   47
5   Student Agency   57
6   Student-Driven Learning   69
7   Creating an Ecosystem for Student-Driven Learning   87

About the Authors   95

Foreword

Joe DiMartino and Jay Midwood have presented a unique approach to school redesign that puts students at the center of attention and then gathers a whole community to conduct inquiry and experimentation that improve performance. The book includes a mass of connected strategies for developing student-driven learning, but the authors focus less on particular strategies than on changing the culture of schools in ways that let both students and professionals learn together how to change their conditions.

While students are learning to manage independent inquiry, adults are also learning how to increase student engagement—studying how changing conditions changes the way students learn. The book prepares members of a school community to collaborate over several years to develop, test, and revise teaching and learning to improve community engagement and student performance.

Rather than dwelling on mechanics, writers DiMartino and Midwood propose an organic approach to school redesign, based on seeing the school as a living ecology, a system of interacting parts that have to evolve in concert to make a lasting difference in the school experience. Understanding school ecology enables all members of a school community, including students, to understand school context, collaborate effectively on project initiatives, and connect their discoveries to the broader effort. Over time schoolwide inquiry transforms school.

The ecological approach to change described and illustrated by the authors is not derived from abstract theories, but from intensive work with many different schools across the United States—all working to change the conditions that currently limit the growth of younger and adult members of the community.

From more than twenty years of extensive and varied collaboration with schools, the authors have identified five essential elements that have to receive continuous attention as a school transforms itself. For each element, the writers provide a range of strategies promoting instructional and organizational adaptation on behalf of student-driven learning. They provide a range of examples showing how those strategies have worked in different settings.

They begin by showing how members of a school community can come to understand their own ecosystem, so change in one area provokes change in connected areas. Within a living ecosystem, the writers show how a restrictive school can develop a culture of inquiry in which adults and students generate important questions, and then go about answering those questions for themselves and for others working on related tasks. Summer institutes, shadowing studies, and team projects, for example, bring adults and young people together to work on issues central to continuous growth.

A few workshops cannot change a culture or carry out adaptive change in one sweep. Instead, building healthy and energetic networks creates coordinated growth, working across the lines that often divide schools into silos. Wide participation in change increases leadership density. Because a school is an interacting network, schools must learn to develop into a fluid kind of organization in which "positional authority" makes way for interactive leadership, shifting responsibilities among participants—or partners, as the authors point out—as exploration reveals opportunities for growth.

Focusing on problems they share, students and teachers expand their sense of personal agency, replacing feelings of personal helplessness with purposeful inquiry. As students begin to understand and respect their own personal agency, they discover their interests and experiences can influence what, how, and where they can learn important skills and ideas.

Years of promising but narrowly conceived fads—in areas such as high-stakes testing, cooperative learning, and alternative school structures, for example—have proven disappointing, because they do not respond to all the pressures and opportunities that have frozen in place long-standing traditions that prevent transformation. Any promising innovation can find a place in changing the conditions of a school, but separate initiatives thrive when the school community adopts them as parts of an ongoing, whole-school transformation.

This book aims to empower all members of a school culture to change existing conditions for their mutual benefit. Reading this book surely reveals ways to manage student-driven learning and improve performance, but more important, it will raise the confidence and awareness of people who may need to try several approaches as they take responsibility for enriching their own experience of life and learning in school.

John H. Clarke
professor emeritus, University of Vermont

Preface

Joseph DiMartino

"I'm not stupid!" That comment is representative of one of the most heart-wrenching and memorable conversations of my life.

It was a month after his return that he came into our sitting room and made the emphatic statement: "I'm not stupid!" To which we responded almost in unison, "We know that, Erick." We were incredulous that Erick had apparently thought he was stupid in the past.

Erick thought we were dismissing him so he repeated the statement, this time a little more loudly. "I really mean it. I'm not stupid." To which we responded, also a little louder, "We really mean it. We know that."

We sat there silently as he questioned, "Then why did they make me feel so stupid at the other high school?" The anguish in the room after that statement was palpable. Pat and I were speechless. We had not realized just what a profound impact his earlier high school experience had on him.

That conversation took place over twenty years ago. Since that time, I have been on a personal and professional journey to better understand why Erick felt so stupid and what happened at his new school that convinced him otherwise. I knew the teachers from his original high school well enough to know that they didn't intend to make him feel stupid. But I've learned over the past two decades that America's high schools unintentionally fail many students. And I have devoted my life to understanding why and to assisting secondary schools in implementing changes so that they wouldn't be places where some (perhaps many?) students learned that they were stupid.

My journey has turned into a quest to help traditional secondary schools become student centered so that all students are known, respected, and valued. *Schools that unleash the basic goodness and genius of each and every student.*

I am convinced that the teachers and administrators at Erick's high school didn't realize the effect that the school organization and culture had on so many students. They didn't realize that, as some students excelled, some, like Erick, struggled to learn in a classroom where instruction delivered through a lecture is the norm. Over two decades, I have come to realize that the conditions that Erick faced in his original high school are the norm throughout the entire country. There are many who believe that the high school is broken and that the people who work in them are slackers or incapable.

Jay Midwood and I have been collaborating on this effort to assist schools and districts to bring about transformational change for the past decade. Together we have written this book—a reflection on how to re-create the American secondary school as a place where learning can happen anytime, anyplace; a place where students demonstrate learning through complex, rigorous performance assessments. Our redesigned high school is a place where teachers function more as facilitators and coaches of learning than as lecturers and dispensers of knowledge. Through a unique opportunity to be engaged with incredible educators from across the country, we have confirmed that *when students are given the opportunity to participate in inquiry-based learning experiences tied to performance assessments, they experience success in school and are better prepared for college and/or career experiences.*

We have confirmed our belief—and now believe even more strongly—that a network of schools could support each other in the development of personalized learning environments that include performance assessments as a vehicle of demonstrating mastery of course competencies. In this model, learning and assessment are inquiry based and personalized for each student, including measures of evidence of achievement that are both reliable and valid.

We are delighted to share with a wider audience what we have learned, what we have created, and how we did it, so that others can draw on our experience to advance their own high school redesign efforts.

Acknowledgments

We are incredibly thankful to a network of educators who have supported our work and whose reflections have helped us bring coherence to this volume. We certainly could not have created this vision of a path to transformation without their guidance and input. They include a national cadre of school change coaches from the Center for Secondary School Redesign: Bill Bryan, Tony Ferreira, Margaret MacLean, Arnie Clayton, Richard Dubuisson, Nelson Beaudoin, Meg Maccini, Dorothy Bowen, Don Siviski, George McDonough, Jan Struebing, Keith Pfeiffer, Keisha Taylor, Lou Constantino, Marsha Jones, Pat DiMartino, Anna Fazekas, John Freeman, Tobi Chasse, Susan Bradley, and Mike Nast.

Teacher to Teacher coaches: Joanna Dolgin, Diane Kruse, Ruth Whalen-Crockett, Lorin Hill, Sue Massocco, Chris Geraghty, and Hannah Kehn.

Leaders of the New England Network for Personalization and Performance (NENPP), especially Paul Leather, and Plymouth Public School Leadership: Gary Maestas, Chris Campbell, and Sean Halpin.

Members of the NENPP Performance Assessment Review Board: Melissa Roderick, Karin Hess, Gregg Sinner, Dick Kraemer, Fred Bramante, Paul Leather, Mariane Gfroerer, Larry Myatt, Wayne Ogden, Linda Nathan, Ryan Champeau, and Peggy Reynolds.

A team from UCLA Center X: Renie Avery, Lisa DiMartino, Jason Cervonce, and Juan Lopez.

We owe a great deal of thanks to Jane Feinberg, who helped us organize our thoughts into the framework presented here.

We are also very thankful for funds provided by the Rural School and Community Trust, the Nellie Mae Education Foundation, and the United States Department of Education.

Chapter One

The Ecosystem of Student-Driven Learning

It has been over three decades since *Horace's Compromise: The Dilemma of the American High School* was first published. In it, Ted Sizer, the author (and a mentor of ours), describes the compromises that Horace Smith was forced to make in his twenty-eight-year career as a high school teacher. Sizer's description of a day in the life of Horace Smith is a dreary account of the real challenges faced in America's high school classrooms for both teachers and students. What's appalling is that despite the acknowledgment that secondary schools are not meeting the needs of most of their students, the middle and high schools in this country have not made any substantial change to personalize learning, teaching, and assessment so that all their students achieve. On the back cover of the 2004 updated publication of *Horace's Compromise*, Debbie Meier writes:

> The book that changed my life. Ted Sizer not only makes us stop and realize what appalling institutions we had created. He did more. The book turned many of us on to creating real schools that "walked the talk" he offered us. Sizer changed not only the conversation about schooling, but schooling itself for thousands of young people and their compromised teachers. Hurrah for re-publishing this extraordinary book.

Debbie is correct in that *Horace's Compromise* led to the creation of schools like the Big Picture Schools modeled after the Met in Providence, High Tech High in San Diego, Fenway High in Boston, and numerous new charter schools across the country. Unfortunately, the success of these start-up schools hasn't changed schooling for most adolescents who are still stuck in

1

traditional schools that are very much like the ones Sizer visited back in the 1980s.

An important method of exploring the culture of a school from a student's perspective is allowing a team of educators from within a school to shadow students. This experience routinely results in making the shadowers aware of the incredibly boring and often demeaning situations that students face each day. The experience is not unlike those described in *Horace's Compromise*.

An effective shadowing experience involves teams of educators from within a school who spend an entire day in the shoes of specific students. The shadowers are challenged in that they must do everything the student they're shadowing has to do. If the student needs to get a pass to go the bathroom, the shadower needs one, too. If the student is asked to sit and take notes, they should sit and take notes. If the student is asked to go to the dean's office for a discipline infraction, the shadower must go with him or her. The team of shadowers will come together at the end of the day to collectively debrief their experience and discuss what changes should take place to improve the culture and learning at the school.

Comments from shadowers during the debrief always point out that something needs to be changed. The comments offered during these sessions are very similar to what Horace Smith offered in the 1980s. A thoughtful and highly regarded teacher offered, "I thought each fifty-minute class seemed like three hours! But when I teach the classes go by in a blur." A new principal offered, "I know that you challenged me to shadow the student for the entire day, but I just couldn't make it. Halfway through the last period of the day, I returned to my office, turned off the lights and sat there pondering what a disservice we are doing to our kids."

The changes suggested by *Horace's Compromise* and made clear by Debbie Meier are real. There are indeed numerous schools that provide true quality educational experience for their students. These schools are nearly all pilot or charter schools. The bigger challenge is how to bring about change to the traditional high schools where most students are enrolled. This book offers insights gained over several years. It provides substantial examples of schools that have made significant shifts in their culture to make school more engaging and provide their students with better opportunities for graduation from high school prepared for life beyond it.

The experiences of the past three decades had left the presumption that school redesign can't happen in already existing comprehensive high schools. The argument has been that if you want to make real change, start your own school. While it seems expedient to follow this path, two decades of pursuing change by building new schools has left the majority of high school students trapped in traditional settings that have continued to provide less than adequate educational opportunities for the vast majority of adolescents.

The challenge facing America's high schools is how best to support change in the schools that most of our young people actually attend. There are schools across the country demonstrating real change in existing environments under the right circumstances. Making these changes may take more time and entail accepting the fact that each school's unique culture requires a unique journey to transformation.

The needed change requires that school-based stakeholders, including students, must move from their traditional ways to transformational ones. This entails questioning their daily habits, routines, practices, processes, and systems—checking them against what a student-centered—and student-driven—environment truly demands. Rather than working to implement a set of short-term technical solutions, successfully transformed schools engage in generating adaptive solutions—that is, solutions that change the very nature of doing business.

The chart in figure 1.1 captures the Center for Secondary School Redesign (CSSR) model's best practices (the "what" is in the far left column) that characterize three levels of school personalization, in other words, *traditional, transitional,* and *transformational.* The numbers between the elements of the continua indicate the level of effort required to make the change from one level to the next: **1 = Relatively Easy; 2 = Moderately Difficult; 3 = Very Difficult**.

Stuck with unacceptable levels of aggregate levels of student progress data as many are, American schools are due for a major "redesigning" effort. The one-size-fits-all curriculum and lockstep schedules allow little if any flexibility for greater personalization of learning, teaching, and assessment. A changing world requires a new kind of educational delivery system. Using the continua shown in figure 1.1 provides the guidance school communities can use to move transformation.

It is exciting to report here how schools across the country have been able to achieve new levels of excellence. All were very tempted to do it quickly, but learned early on that they had to "go slow, to go fast" to be successful. In other words, the importance of process, planning, and intentionality around goals cannot be overstated. Just as an inquiry-based classroom puts a premium on the teacher as the facilitator of knowledge who creates framework and structures, our work has provided the same kind of scaffolding for schools, keeping in mind the motto "heart before head, touch before task, and relationship before rigor."

What resulted was meaningful growth, regardless of the inevitable changes in staff and administration. Each school developed its own new way of doing business that aligned with the central value proposition of the vision

Traditional (industrial model) → *Transitional* (teacher-centered model) → *Transformational* (student-centered model)

A. STUDENT AGENCY

	Traditional	Rating	Transitional	Transformational
2-Student	Passive Recipient/Compliant	3	Engaged	Passion and Self-Direction
3-Class Climate	Teacher Control	2	Some Shared Ownership	Positive & Student-Led/Managed
4-Personalization	Parent-Teacher Conferences	2	Student-Led Conferences	Student Exhibitions
5-Governance	Student Council	2	Rep Democratic Structures	Student-Led Site Council

D. CULTURE OF INQUIRY

	Traditional	Rating	Transitional	Transformational
1-Teacher Role	Instructor	3	Instructor/Advisor	Facilitator/Advisor/Coach
3-Framework	Assessment of Learning	1	Assessment for Learning	Assessment as Learning
4-Type Assessment	High-Stakes Assessment	2	Structured Perform Assessment	Personalized Performance
7-Develop Vehicle	Recertification Hours: 3 Years	3	Common Plng Time/Grp Learning	Collaborative Inquiry

B. POWER OF NETWORK

	Traditional	Rating	Transitional	Transformational
3-Accountability	Student	3	Teacher	Learning Team
4-Prof Culture	Faculty Meetings	2	Prof Learning Community	Focus Empowered Groups
5-Parents	Passive/Not Engaged	2	Attend Events	Full Partner
6-Community	Compliance	2	Cooperation & Provide Resources	Collaboration & Full Partner

C. STUDENT-DRIVEN LEARNING

	Traditional	Rating	Transitional	Transformational
3-Personalization	Group Instruction	1	Differentiation	Student Choice/PPP
4-Learning Locus	Classroom	2	School	Anywhere/Anyplace
5-Timeframe	8 a.m.–2 p.m.	2	Before School/8–2/After School	Anytime
6-Content Vehicle	Text-Driven Instruction	2	Competency & Pjct-Based Instruct	Demonstration of Mastery
9-Curric Impetus	Teacher/Content	3	Inquiry/Essential Questions	Performance-Based Assessment

E. SHARED LEADERSHIP

	Traditional	Rating	Transitional	Transformational
1-Vision	Nonexistent/Fragmented	2	Some on Same Page	Common & Compelling Vision
8-Students	Student Groups/Teams Only	2	Some Inclusion & Training	Leadership Role on Most Teams
11-Communication	Fragmented or Wrong Focus	1	Some Processes in Place	Fully Integrated Processes
12-Buy-in	Little Focus	2	Some Attention Paid/Reactive	Proactive Sophist Influence Plans
13-Teams	Loosely Structured	3	Disciplined Structure & Meetings	Chartered Engines of Change
14-Role Clarity	Limited & Haphazard	1	Some Role/Job Definition	Fully Defined/Vetted Jobs/Roles

Figure 1.1. CSSR's model best practices continua.

that students should be at the center of their own learning and the drivers of their own educational experiences.

These schools were guided by a re-visioning of the American high school as a place where learning can happen anytime, anyplace; a place where students demonstrate learning through complex, rigorous performance assessments. The redesigned high school is a place where teachers function more as facilitators and coaches of learning than as lecturers and dispensers of knowledge. *Students who participate in inquiry-based learning experiences tied to performance assessments will experience success in school and be better prepared for college and/or career experiences.*

* * *

Accomplishing this kind of systemic and sustainable change for all students requires that schools focus on five different elements in an ecosystem of change. We examined reflections from schools that have successfully implemented these changes—including thoughts expressed by students, teachers, and school and district leaders, as well as coaches from the Center for Secondary School Redesign. From these conversations, we created framework that captured the core elements of effective high school redesign. This framework is an ecosystem of student-driven learning, where each of five major elements working together will lead to school change that is meaningful. *Each of the elements on its own can bring about positive change for students.* However, to bring about lasting school change, all five elements should work together. The interconnectivity of elements is shown in figure 1.2.

CULTURE OF INQUIRY

A "culture of inquiry" is a set of conditions that exist within a school and its district in which the focus of the learning for students and adults centers on answering important and compelling questions. *The culture of inquiry exists on two levels: with students at the classroom level, and with educators at the school level.* In the classroom, it is evident through flexibility in the curriculum as it is driven by student questions as well as a list of content that has been covered.

In a culture of inquiry, students and teachers collaborate to create the teaching and learning experience. Student questions emerge in the context of the curriculum and goals of the class. Students are at the center of all learning activities and have the ability to connect their passions with "uncommon" learning tasks. Uncommon learning tasks are self-driven and individually designed to connect with their personal passions and interests, and are assessed against a working rubric that is common across all students working toward demonstration of mastery of core competencies.

Culture of Inquiry	Power of Network	Shared Leadership	Student Agency	Student Driven Learning
A set of conditions that exist within a school or district in which the focus of learning for students and adults is around answering important and compelling questions	Intentional design choices to harness the power of networking—employing skilled facilitative leadership to support each site.	Creating leadership "density"—beyond those in "positional" authority—can greatly accelerate the change process.	A set of conditions in which students are empowered to become key partners in the decision-making process about issues that affect their daily experiences in school.	Schools must create a set of conditions in which students are empowered to become key partners in the decision-making process about issues that affect their daily experiences in school.

Figure 1.2.   Ecosystem of student learning.

It is important to note that in a culture of inquiry, students are still held to the established standards or competencies; pursuing those learning outcomes through an inquiry-based process provides a better method for understanding and retaining new knowledge. For example, a teacher asked students to create a chemistry question of interest to them personally. One student said he wondered if the stream behind his house was polluted. The teacher and the class collaborated and agreed to explore a class inquiry question: "Is the stream behind David's house polluted?" In the course of the investigation, students addressed numerous required Next Generation Science Standards for chemistry and demonstrated several of the required competencies.

At the school level, a culture of inquiry promotes purposeful collaboration, instead of siloed practice. Faculty and administrators seek answers to important and relevant questions about their practice using student data in a cycle of inquiry to inform their work. It is a powerful model of authentic learning for both students and adults.

POWER OF A NETWORK

Intentional networks became an important venue for fostering a supportive system of sharing knowledge, information, and expertise. The power of collaboration—the power of a network—is finding ways to constantly learn from each other.

To change school culture, we must question the traditional philosophy of "my kids, my classroom." For far too long, educators have operated within the confines of their four classroom walls in what one site coordinator called "pure isolation." In order to make the transformational shift toward student-driven learning, schools and districts are required to make intentional design choices to harness the power of networking, and employ skilled facilitative leadership to support each site in accomplishing grant goals.

Through a collaborative process and multiple learning opportunities for teachers, students, and school administrators, schools are able to move out of isolation and become a community of learners. Through this experience, they explore new horizons in teaching and learning, including inquiry-based instruction that supports student agency and student-designed learning experiences. By creating opportunities for site teams to develop strategies and support structures, they are able to examine their own professional development through reflection, refinement, and skill building. Over time, site teams become the drivers of change where stakeholders feel comfortable taking risks and trying new strategies.

> "It is really nice to see what other schools are doing and to learn from our school change coaches who always came in with an eye towards development and change. I highly encourage more schools to engage in the networking process because it is comforting to know I can pick up the phone and call a colleague in another state and say 'we are struggling with something; how did you guys do it?' That outside lens would help us when we felt like we were getting caught up not being able to see the forest through the trees. The conversation would just help us see things differently."—Peggy Reynolds, site coordinator, Nashua High School North and South

SHARED LEADERSHIP

When we think of leaders, we typically imagine an individual or individuals who are positioned at the top of a hierarchy—or "positional leaders." Recognizing that this traditional definition of leadership exists in most organizations, and that effective "positional" leadership is, indeed, critical to school change, a broader definition of leadership that is shared and distributed is necessary to bring about real, sustained change.

Leadership can pop up in the most surprising places in an organization, and leadership "density" can greatly accelerate the change process. Exemplary leadership can emerge from teachers, site coordinators, administrators, students, parents, and community members. Having leaders across the organization and community is perhaps the most effective way of ensuring that change will "stick" because many people own it. Shared leadership focuses on fostering communication, cooperation, and collaboration in an organization, and is built on a commitment to realizing both individual and organizational goals. Creating conditions for individuals to feel that they are listened to and taken seriously by positional leaders is a success factor for developing effective shared leadership.

Shared leadership is especially important in high-demand environments like a school, in which there are many moving parts and in which all of the parts are interconnected in some way. Distributing the leadership across the organization requires a level of sophistication and proficiency that has not previously been expected of those who work in schools. A student-driven environment requires that new leadership skills be developed across the organization. In essence, shared leadership changes the culture—the values, norms, and deeply held beliefs that are beneath the surface of day-to-day behavior. The following core elements of shared leadership serve as the enablers to authentic culture change:

Students. Students are taken seriously and are fully engaged in school change and viewed as partners in the redesign process—having a role on most leadership teams.

Compelling vision. All stakeholders are working in unison toward common and innovative student outcomes.

Collaboration and communication. Formal mechanisms are in place to provide the entire school community with regular opportunities for structured collaboration.

Influence and energy. School leaders prioritize initiatives and best practices in a way that focuses energy and influence toward the activities that have the greatest impact on student achievement.

Capacity building. Teachers, students, and administrators are not only focusing on tangible classroom practices, but also cultivating the intrinsic behaviors that will sustain change and continue to develop relationships over time.

Developing leadership skills among stakeholders happens over time—not through one or two workshops or trainings. It requires an adaptive philosophy and an ability to mobilize people to meet a set of goals and embrace a set of challenges. Tending to the little habits, routines, practices and processes, and systems of student-driven learning builds people's sense of efficacy, and can spark significant changes in the school culture. *Simply designating individuals as leaders, without directed professional development to give them the tools and authority necessary to act on their own, will do nothing but create resentment and chaos.*

STUDENT AGENCY

How do learning environments embrace student agency in a way that allows students to create their own pathways and be engaged, allowing the deepest learning and involvement possible?

The irony of school life is that the students and the teachers at the center of the educational enterprise are the least empowered members of the community. Without opportunities for students and teachers to develop and use their own voices and influence what learning could look like in their communities, students will have an educational experience that lacks substance, purpose, and relevance. *In order to better serve students, schools must create a set of conditions in which students are empowered to become key partners in the decision-making process about issues that affect their daily experiences in school.*

In the ideal student-centered environment, student input is sought, listened to, and addressed authentically. Programs, organizations, and structures in the school share the vision that all students deserve the opportunity to have voice and choice, and recognize that young people are capable of participating, leading, and taking action in the school community. Students can become the chief architects of their learning and contributing citizens of the school community. Schools that embrace student agency drastically improve learning environments where teachers are facilitators of knowledge, skills, and talent development and all students are prepared for life after high school.

Student agency is based on the idea that every student can uniquely contribute to the successful transformation of the learning community if given the right opportunities. The following conditions promote the development of student agency in the classroom:

Opportunities to develop and express a personal voice. Students must have the chance to express their ideas as they gradually form and engage in dialogue that can connect different perspectives and facilitate new solutions to challenges in the learning environment.

Chance to belong to a working group. Students are empowered when working with other individuals—teachers and students—to effect positive change in the learning environment.

Adult advocates. A productive relationship with a trusted adult is critical for students to feel known and valued in their school.

Learning choice. Students increase their sense of personal competence through a variety of experiences both in and out of the classroom. Students have the opportunity to decide what they learn, and how they learn it. Connecting these varied learning experiences helps students build value and direction for their personal paths.

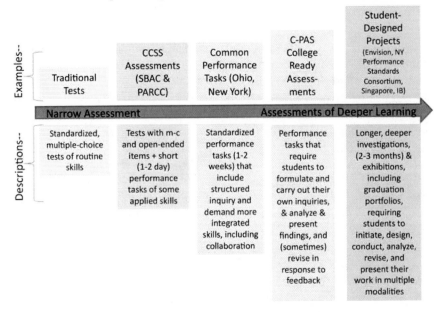

Figure 1.3. Assessment continuum.

STUDENT-DRIVEN LEARNING

The guiding principles of student-driven learning are:

- The learning and teaching is structured around the concept that students bring into the learning environment their unique experiences (tangible and intangible) and strengths to build upon and contribute to their own learning.
- Each student has the opportunity to learn through flexible times and opportunities; the development of extended learning opportunities (ELOs) begins with student passions and desires.
- Performance assessments are at the core of putting students at the center of their own learning. At the heart of this work are projects that are student generated.
- The learning in and out of the classroom is collaborative in nature and includes regularly structured opportunities for reflection, feedback, and refinement.
- Moderation of student scores is the vehicle to ensure that the deepest learning possible is occurring; a vehicle for demonstration of knowledge.

- The learning is deeper, as students demonstrate mastery through a competency-based approach. Personalized exhibitions, portfolios, and other gateways require students to initiate, design, conduct, analyze, revise, and present their work in multiple ways; there is common scoring for uncommon learning tasks.

This book can be used as a professional development guide, but it will also serve as a vehicle to provide a better understanding of personalized learning.

Table 1.1. Adapting Five Elements of School Culture to Promote Student-Driven Learning (Focusing idea: *Within the ecosystem of a changing school, five elements interact to activate improvement in learning and teaching by working together to change the school culture.***)**

Five Elements Promoting Change	Professional Development	Personalized Student Learning
*A culture of inquiry—*teachers and students actively engaged in learning to manage the school context	Focuses on compelling questions that have to be answered cooperatively as school-wide culture evolves	Focuses on "real" problems and questions that students regard as important to themselves and their community
*Power of networks—*the work of teachers and students linked in ways that change school culture	Connects individual interests to a planned network of team initiatives that interact to change school culture	Organizes student inquiry so individuals and teams deeply explore important questions and propose workable answers
*Shared leadership—*shifting patterns of leadership that adapt as situations change and individuals learn	Shifts responsibility for linked initiatives to students and adults who then become responsible for change	Creates roles for each student essential to gathering information and proposing answers or novel ideas
*Student agency—*empowering individuals to pursue learning that changes their conditions	Frees adults to include students in the design of workable solutions to shared problems they all face within their schools	Frees students to gather information from diverse sources and apply it to "real" situations
*Student-driven learning—*validation of life experiences that support personal learning in pursuit of applicable knowledge	Supports teachers and administrators who use personal learning to create change for the school community	Celebrates the strategies students develop to follow their interests and manage their learning so knowledge "works"
*Final word—*ongoing adaptation, taking us from where we are to where we need to be	Presents an array of coherent strategies for creating a learning community that responds to emerging conditions	Prepares students and adults to see how their learning can improve their lives and the vitality of their communities

Chapter Two

Culture of Inquiry

A culture of inquiry is a set of conditions that exists within a school or a district in which the focus of the learning for students and adults centers on answering important and compelling questions.

Jenny Wellington, an English teacher at Pittsfield Middle High School in Pittsfield, New Hampshire, has embraced inquiry-based pedagogy in her classroom. She recently reflected on how starting with the questions and not the answer has resulted in tremendous gains for her students. She seems to have been astounded when she offers that "it's amazing that when you want their input and give them the chance to design it with you how their motivation goes up, their interest goes up and the product they create is stronger."

Instead of giving them what she wants them to get out of a text, she approaches her class with the question "what did you get from this text?" In her words, "By starting with the questions I just gave you something to read, what do you think about it? The conversation always gets around to what I wanted them to think about and more often than not goes beyond."[1]

DEVELOPING INQUIRY-BASED TEACHING PRACTICES

Creating inquiry-based classrooms is a good place to begin to change the school culture to get to the deepest learning possible. Inquiry-based instruction cultivates critical habits of mind that transcend any particular discipline. When students experience learning as a process of posing and seeking answers to interesting questions, they also learn *how to learn*. Inquiry in the classroom expects them to be active agents in their own education, while teaching and reinforcing skills needed for success in our increasingly complex society. This was particularly true in the New England Network for Personalization and Performance, a network of schools across four states, as teachers from many different disciplines embraced this approach and created new levels of engagement for their students. Many educators saw a shift in their role from provider of information, to facilitator of learning.

To be fully effective, inquiry-based classrooms need to exist within a "culture of inquiry." The culture of inquiry exists at two levels: with students at the classroom level, and with educators at the school level. In the classroom, it is evident through flexibility in the curriculum as it is driven by student questions rather than a list of content that has been covered.

When a culture of inquiry is in place, teaching and learning is co-constructed by both students and teachers, and is motivated by authenticity and questions that both kids and adults want answered. Students are at the center of all learning activities and have the ability to connect their passions with "uncommon" learning tasks. These uncommon learning tasks are self-driven and individually designed to connect with their personal passions and interests, but are assessed against a working rubric that is common across all students as they work toward a demonstration of mastery of core competencies.

It is important to note that in a culture of inquiry, students are still held to the established standards or competencies; pursuing those learning outcomes through an inquiry-based process provides a better method for understanding and retaining new knowledge.

At the school level, a culture of inquiry promotes purposeful collaboration, instead of siloed practice. Faculty and administrators seek answers to important and relevant questions about their practice using student data in a cycle of inquiry to inform their work. It is a powerful model of authentic learning for both students and adults.

When schools adopt a culture of inquiry, the learning for students and adults is equally significant and powerful. The schools that make the greatest strides toward creating a culture of inquiry have done so through the following three avenues, each of which is elaborated on later in this chapter.

- Developing inquiry-based teaching practices in the classroom.
- Using a cycle of inquiry as a model for teacher collaboration.
- Engaging all stakeholders.

GETTING STARTED

What can educators do to begin the transition to more inquiry-based teaching practices? Educators should start by gaining a better understanding of the experience of the students in their own schools and how best to meet student needs and aspirations. Engaging in student shadowing, student forums, and other culture and climate evaluations to gather this information provides schools with a better understanding of why this change needs to take place.

What can educators and schools do to promote a culture of inquiry? "Shadow students" is the advice that Linda Chick, site coordinator at Manchester High School West in Manchester, New Hampshire, suggests. Principal Chris Motika went on to say "You have to see the school from the student's perspective; it is an eye-opener. Let the teachers and students determine what comes next [in your transformational change], but it is critical that any shift in culture starts with them."[2]

STUDENT SHADOWING TO LAY THE GROUNDWORK FOR INQUIRY

The purpose of shadowing is for school leaders to see the school from the students' perspective so that they may better prepare classroom and school side discussions that are guided by the student experience in their school. This greatly enhances the perspective of adults on ways to make things better for students.

To be certain to gain a full understanding of the student experience, a team of shadowers must be created that is composed of ten to twelve individuals—at least one administrator, preferably two students, and teachers representing various constituencies in the school. It's our experience that the student day tends to be seen as very boring by the shadowers, so an outside facilitation might be incorporated to help to ensure that the shadowing debrief doesn't become a dispiriting exercise.

Students assigned to be shadowed should represent all of the possible tracks within the school. Team members should be assigned to shadow students they don't see in the normal course of their day. For example, special education teachers might be assigned a student who has a number of AP classes or teachers of AP might be assigned students in a general track. The purpose is to expand everyone's understanding of all the different educational programs in the school from the perspective of the student.

This exercise is not about evaluating individual teachers; rather, it's designed to give the school's leadership team a better sense of the needs of the students in the school. Figures 2.1 and 2.2 outline the CSSR student shadowing protocol.

Over more than a decade, Center for Secondary School Redesign (CSSR) coaches have facilitated student shadowing, including lengthy, sometimes intense, debrief conversations to learn from the findings of student shadowers. These conversations should inform professional learning communities (PLCs) tasked with addressing the gaps in practice revealed by the shadowing. From there, teachers began using the cycle of inquiry to address barriers

CSSR: Protocol for Student Shadowing

The purpose of shadowing is for school leaders to see the school from the students' perspective so that they may better prepare a smaller learning community initiative that is indeed focused on making things better for students.

The leadership team MUST be comprised of 10 to 12 individuals—at least one administrator, preferably two students, and the balance teachers representing various constituencies in the school. Two CSSR facilitators will also shadow students.

Students assigned to be shadowed should represent all of the possible tracks within the school. Leadership team members will be assigned to shadow students that they don't see in the normal course of their day. For example, special Ed teachers might be assigned a student that has a number of AP classes or Teachers of AP might be assigned students in a general track. The purpose is to expand everyone's understanding of all the different educational programs in the school from the perspective of the student.

This exercise is not about evaluating any individual teachers, but rather it's designed to give the smaller learning communities leadership team a better sense of the needs of the students in the school.

Guidance for Shadowers:

- Greet the student assigned to you as soon as he or she enters school.

- Introduce yourself and make sure the student understands that you will accompany him or her throughout the entire day.

- Introduce your self to any your student's friends that you meet during the course of the day.

Figure 2.1. Student shadowing protocol, page 1.

- As you enter each classroom be sure that the teacher understands that you are not their to evaluate them in any way but that you are there as part of a needs assessment for the federal smaller learning community initiative. Ask them to treat you as any other student and not to alter their plans for the class in any way.

- Do everything the student does during the entire day. If the student is expected to sit quietly and take notes, you do likewise. It's not okay to get lunch at some other time or place than the students or to stand outside of the classroom at any time during the class. If students can't have impromptu conversations with teachers than neither can you.

- In each class sit as close to your student as you can without disrupting the class.

- You must follow the rules established for student behavior. If passes are needed to go the bathroom, you will need to obtain a pass.

- Lunch is a great opportunity to get the student perspective about their school. Ask them and their friends any questions that might help to clarify some issues that have entered your mind up to that time. It is usually helpful to ask if this is a typical day at the school and how it might be different on other days.

- Take notes of what you observe during the course of the day. Be prepared to give the balance of the leadership team a brief summary of your observations. Be sure your report does not identify any individual teachers.

Figure 2.2. Student shadowing protocol, page 2.

to full-scale implementation of a culture of inquiry. As critical as it is to *begin* this transformational change with students, schools also must *continuously collaborate* with students in the transition to inquiry-based teaching practices and *regularly review* artifacts of student learning as part of the cycle of inquiry (described later in the chapter).

For many teachers, a safe entry point was learning to develop strong essential questions and good questioning techniques to drive learning in the classroom. A number of teachers used the question formulation technique from the Right Question Institute to jumpstart their work.

In addition, teachers can view videos of classroom practice, develop and tune inquiry-based lessons and assessments, and practice using protocols to facilitate substantive conversations regarding change in practice. Students' voices must be included in all the conversations regarding the transition to inquiry-based teaching. Students usually provide authentic feedback on their instructional needs and desires, their visions for what inquiry-based teaching practices could look like in their classrooms, and their ideas about what their role could be in the learning process.

TEACHER COLLABORATION AND THE CYCLE OF INQUIRY

For schools to adopt a true culture of inquiry, the transformative practices cannot be limited to interactions with students in the classroom. In order for it to become part of the fabric of a school or district, the leadership and faculty must embrace the same facets of inquiry learning as the students. The work of teachers must be (1) to establish the right structures to sustain collaborative practices, and (2) use these structures to engage in a cycle of inquiry focused on student data for the purposes of improving teaching and learning and increasing student achievement.

CREATING A PROFESSIONAL LEARNING COMMUNITY THROUGH COLLABORATIVE STRUCTURES

One of the most basic and powerful ways to create and sustain collaborative structures in schools is to create a faculty of trained professionals who engage with one another regularly. Their collaboration includes guided discussions and activities to examine student work using vetted calibration or validation protocols. This requires that schools create an environment for purposeful and courageous conversations around professional practice and teacher behaviors. CSSR offers a five-day collaborative skills and practices (CSP) training that is designed to: support the development of a truly collaborative school community; promote reflective practice; and encourage facilitative leadership—with an ultimate goal of increasing student achievement.

"Teachers have to begin thinking about collaboration differently; teachers must begin to experience positive collaboration with their team of colleagues or content experts. They must begin to shift the culture to a non-hierarchical structure. It is hard work."—CSSR coach Margaret MacLean

CYCLE OF INQUIRY

Collaborative structures provide the right foundation for school teams to engage in a cycle of inquiry in which student and other pertinent school or district data are used to answer important and compelling questions brought forth by teachers and administrators. Educators and students in the i3 New England Network used the cycle of inquiry to have interdisciplinary conversations focused on specific artifacts of student work that would engage teachers to improve inquiry within the classroom and throughout the entire learning community.

In a cycle of inquiry (figure 2.3), teachers begin by coming together around a key problem of practice. Teachers then gather appropriate data that they analyze using structured protocols to help them develop a better understanding of their problem. From there, they develop a strategy and plan of action to begin addressing the issue. Finally, teachers analyze new data to see what impact their strategy has had on the problem of practice. Because it is a cycle, the inquiry continues by raising additional questions that build off the original problem of practice, or arise as a result of new strategies.

Collaborative structures, including the cycle of inquiry, are an invaluable tool for schools moving toward a culture of inquiry. For such transformational changes to take place, educators must de-privatize their practice as they develop new lessons, calibrate assessment tools, validate summative assessments, and continuously look at student work with their colleagues as part of the data analysis portion of the inquiry cycle.

DEVELOPING INQUIRY-BASED TEACHING PRACTICES

Inquiry-based instruction cultivates critical habits of mind that transcend any particular discipline. When students experience learning as a process of posing interesting questions and seeking answers to them, they also learn how to learn. Inquiry in the classroom expects them to be active agents in their own education, while teaching and reinforcing skills needed for success in our increasingly complex society.

This is particularly true in schools where teachers from many different disciplines have embraced this approach, have the opportunity to collaboratively plan during common planning time periods, and are deeply committed to creating new levels of engagement for their students. In those environ-

Figure 2.3. Cycle of inquiry.

ments, educators saw a shift in their role from provider of information to facilitator of learning, which is an important dynamic shift that helps students be fully engaged in their learning.

The following section includes stories and strategies of successful implementation in four main content areas: math, English, world languages, and social studies. The lessons contained in these examples can be applied to almost any other content area with a motivated faculty and consistent training and support from leaders with a vision for whole school change.

MAKING STEM COMPELLING

The instructional sequence for STEM instruction in the United States is often *introduce, model, practice*. Application of learning comes after skill development, and most experience is with word problems that involve following examples from very similar problems demonstrated by the teacher, or rote memorization of processes. Application, in this approach, is often more about following steps and recognizing cues and patterns rather than drawing on a knowledge base to really puzzle through a problem.

One major success of this approach has been the broadening of the vision of what rigorous inquiry-based STEM (science, technology, engineering, and mathematics) instruction and assessment *could* look like. Powerful practices that helped STEM teachers cultivate inquiry-based teaching in their classrooms included (1) developing new methods of assessment; (2) teaching through problem solving; (3) promoting classroom discourse and "grit"; and (4) changing the kind of feedback students received.

While many teachers and schools continue to use unit tests and semester exams to assess fluency and understanding of concepts, many successful teachers have adopted new methods for assessing student performance for applied problem solving. Working collaboratively, teachers have developed performance tasks and open-ended problems that required their students to synthesize and apply their learning in novel contexts. Teacher-developed rubrics have been created to define the criteria for quality performance on these tasks. The design of these tasks does not necessarily mean starting from scratch; frequently, the inspiration comes from a problem or lab in the current textbook, and the challenge was to rewrite it so that it became non-routine.

STEM teachers have also worked on shifting instruction from teaching *toward* problems to teaching *through* problem solving. Finding compelling problems to *open* a unit of study is as important as developing high-quality performance tasks—good opening problems "hook" students by engaging them and provoking questions, motivating the need to learn new skills. Direct instruction typically does follow, and includes teacher demonstration and student practice to build fluency. The difference is that the need to learn and practice the skill is motivated by the students' prior experience with the opening problems, and serves to answer a more compelling question.

Inquiry-based STEM instruction means students are more frequently working in small groups arguing their ideas with each other, testing possibilities, proposing alternate approaches, and helping each other understand the content involved. For many teachers, *and students*, these shifts have caused real discomfort. Students were more at ease following steps and working from a clear pattern or demonstration—a common refrain from students is "just show me what to do."

Teachers have had to rethink their assumptions about successful teaching—resisting the urge to explain too quickly, instead working on coaching students to think things through. If educators succumb to the students' stated need for a roadmap, they are doing the thinking, not our students. It is significantly better that we allow them to progress through an ambiguous situation by doing the thinking themselves. Teachers must grapple with student impatience and discomfort that comes with the ambiguity, and encourage students to push through that discomfort to new levels of problem solving.

Inquiry-based teaching requires a different kind of feedback for students. The use of rubrics to assess open-ended problem solving challenges teachers to describe the criteria that define excellent work, rather than use points to give credit or partial credit. For students, this means better, clearer feedback about their performance, shifting their thinking from "did I get the right answer?" to "was I thinking about the problem in a way that made sense, and how can I improve?" This type of feedback yields powerful discussions on student progress and was critical to the success of the new systems of assessment and instruction.

A teacher from Nashua High School North in Nashua, New Hampshire, uses a "calibration protocol" with students in his freshman writing class. In this lesson, students scored actual student work, with the student name redacted, in a different class against an assignment that was common to the students doing the calibrating. By paying particular attention to the calibration process, engaging in the practice of scoring student work can be used across all disciplines to create better inquiry-based learning opportunities.

ENGAGING STUDENTS IN WORLD LANGUAGES

Successful implementation of inquiry-based learning strategies in world languages requires a student-centered classroom where teaching and learning are co-constructed around interesting and level-appropriate questions based on self, and learning activities are immersed in the culture related to the target language. Curriculum design focuses on developing conversation starters rooted in topics that engage and encourage students to talk about self. In an inquiry-based world languages classroom, teachers move away from large survey units on topics such as food or clothing, and instead work to facilitate meaningful conversations driven by student interest.

At Plymouth South High School in Plymouth, Massachusetts, students in a Spanish language classroom suggested exploring America's coffee culture by asking, "Does America really run on Dunkin'?" The classroom teacher wasn't certain if the students wanted to discuss their favorite beverages, describe their dependency on caffeine, or discuss the cultural relevance Dunkin' Donuts coffee has in New England. However, with an intriguing question to guide learning, she was able to trigger language exploration within the scope of students' skills. For example, a new Spanish student would not be able to compare Dunkin' Donuts coffee to coffee brewed at home; however, they could list all the drinks they consumed and share which drink was their favorite. They could also list other drinks and brands present in other areas of New England and the United States.

By beginning with a provocative question, and creating flexible lessons in which students drove the inquiry process, the classroom environment often shifts dramatically. Inquiry-based instruction requires teachers to listen carefully to student responses and allow student conversations to evolve based on student interest. As a result, students develop language skills with real conversation tasks, and are far more competent than their peers who can merely describe the contents of their refrigerator.

World languages teachers can be driven to implement inquiry-based learning strategies out of their students' curiosity about language development and acquisition. Better understanding of how humans learn language facilitates the creation of level-appropriate questions. Teachers have worked to better understand the proficiency and performance standards outlined by the American Council of Teachers of Foreign Languages (ACTFL) and found greatest success when their tasks and questions aligned with the language levels detailed by the ACTFL.

But what does this mean in practice? In the past, teachers often developed the sequence of a lesson or unit based on vocabulary and grammar content. Years of classroom study were predominantly designed on verb tenses and grammatical complexities. By focusing instead on how language is acquired, teachers are using more classroom time to allow lengthy discourse that results in greater conversational competence and comprehension.

PROBING AND PROBLEM SOLVING IN SOCIAL STUDIES

Social studies lends itself particularly well to the culture of inquiry that can be developed in the classroom. A practice central to social studies involves asking compelling questions that demand critical thinking and problem solving related to authentic scenarios. At Kearsarge Regional High School in North Sutton, New Hampshire, American Government teachers have sparked student engagement through the point of inquiry project. This assignment is introduced to students on the first day of class, and they are asked to keep a running list of topics and questions that they have about government as the class progresses. Later in the year, students select a topic of interest from the framework of the structured curriculum in order to create their point of inquiry.

The point of inquiry is a statement or question that drives research and exploration rooted in an area of student interest. By the end of the project, students will research and write an informative paper, and then present findings in small roundtable discussions on their selected topic. The point of inquiry assignment has created increased levels of engagement among students in the American Government course and has the added benefit of exposing all students to a wide array of contemporary issues during the roundtable discussions that take place as a final element of the assessment process.

Early in the year, social studies teachers begin preparing students to complete the point of inquiry project by creating opportunities for students to create compelling questions. Students frequently work in groups to collaboratively generate questions about video segments or pieces of writing they have encountered. The process includes brainstorming ideas and collectively evaluating and improving questions to move away from simple close-ended questions to more dynamic open-ended questions. Such assignments allow students to consider what makes a good question, and in many instances, ultimately drive the selection of their point of inquiry topic.

One example of a unit that prepares students for the point of inquiry project evaluates whether the United States government has remained true to the nation's constitutional principles in dealing with the detention and prosecution of enemy combatants at the military prison in Guantanamo Bay, Cuba. Students start by investigating questions that they create regarding the detention and military commissions taking place in Guantanamo Bay.

After completing their own research, students engage in a class discussion facilitated by the teacher and ultimately write a position paper in response to the following prompt: Assess the level of success that the United States government has achieved in staying true to the nation's constitutional principles in creating the military commissions in Guantanamo Bay, Cuba.

Lessons developed using an inquiry approach, such as the Guantanamo assignment, bring a required unit on constitutional principles to life with a relevant real-world dilemma. Instead of simply memorizing examples of judicial review and checks and balances, students must evaluate how well the government has applied these principles to the difficult issues confronting the war on terror and how these principles should be used in an ever-changing world. As a result, students are better able to participate in our nation's democracy by considering how they want their representatives to apply the constitutional principles to future dilemmas the nation may face.

LEADERSHIP SUPPORT

The involvement of school and district leaders was a critical linchpin for making significant strides toward building a culture of inquiry. For any change initiative to be successful in schools, administrators have to develop a vision for the work as well as a plan for its implementation. School leaders (positional leaders, student leaders, instructional leaders, and culture change leaders) may need support in understanding and adopting several guiding principles for building a culture of inquiry. Leadership mentors can help these leaders build their capacity to lead and sustain the work by engaging multiple stakeholders in the change process. The following guiding principles outline the vision for the culture of inquiry:

- Listen to students and involve them in curricular discussions around learning and teaching. A culture of inquiry begins with understanding how students in your school learn best and what they need to be career and college ready.
- Teachers facilitate learning instead of delivering information. This creates an environment where students feel both empowered and equally responsible for driving the learning in the classroom.
- Students are allowed and expected to complete learning anytime, anyplace, and at any pace. Schools are encouraged to evaluate their structures and systems, including classroom and bell schedules, to ensure they align with the goals of "anyplace, anytime learning." These changes must involve all stakeholders and sometimes challenge local requirements (i.e., seat time).
- Pedagogical changes are driven by students gaining and demonstrating the knowledge, skills, and dispositions needed to be competent and well prepared for life after high school. Inquiry-based learning begins with students asking questions about content, and using the content as an entry point for exploring possible answers to these questions. This process empowers students to take more ownership of the learning while developing the skills with which to do so.
- Assessments guide and inform teaching so that learning opportunities meet the needs of each student. Instruction and assessments can be co-constructed by students and teachers to measure and reinforce content knowledge, skills, and behaviors needed to be successful.
- Students and teachers regularly collaborate and look at student work through moderation, calibration, and validation. Both students and teachers learn through a culture of inquiry. School leaders must foster a collaborative culture among teachers, including by training them to develop the collaborative skills necessary to sustain the work. (More information about moderation, calibration, and validation can be found in chapter 3, "The Power of Network.")

SUPPORT FOR ALL STAKEHOLDERS

In order for schools to successfully create lasting change in classroom practice, school and district leaders have to engage stakeholders in the change process. Whether at the beginning of the process or a short time after the work has begun, a vision for change has to be articulated by school leaders with substantial input from a wide array of community members. All stakeholders must continue to be engaged with the vision and have open conversations about what implementation would mean for everyone. School leaders should also communicate the incentives, resources, and skills needed for the change process, combined with an action plan outlining the steps the school would take to achieve this vision.

This process avoids the "roll-out" phenomenon, in which people feel that something is being done *to* them, not *with* them. It's important to remember that the journey toward change is not a linear one, but that full engagement of those involved enables a school to start where they are and travel where they need to be.

Professional development for teachers and students needs to be ongoing, collaborative, and embedded in the work of the school. This goes beyond workshops and presentations; rather, teachers must be allowed to see and experience different instructional methods, reflect on how those methods might work with their students, and work collaboratively to implement the changes they identified as important to their work.

Teachers can spend substantial time working collaboratively across a network of schools to develop lesson plans and assessments to bring back to their sites, and share these lessons, assessments, and student work with each other in structured sessions. Groups have learned from each other, not just from an "expert" in the room. Professional development should also be focused on shifting beliefs about teaching and learning through courageous conversations that are critical for tackling major change initiatives.

Students, parents, and community members need to understand the changes, and need assurance that even if the new learning environment looked different than what they were accustomed to, students would still be prepared for postsecondary life (even better prepared!). In many schools, leaders have created the conditions for teachers and students to take risks, learn from their triumphs and tribulations, and continuously improve their work—all in a supportive environment. These leaders regularly engage with parents and community members about the changes being contemplated or under way.

The following outlines a proven process for facilitating the development of a culture of inquiry:

Professional development for teachers and students is ongoing, collaborative, and embedded in the work of the school. Summer training should focus not just on learning new techniques, but also on shifting beliefs about teaching and learning. Teachers should revisit these conversations at least annually and spend time working with, and learning from, colleagues in other districts. Under the best conditions, this effort is sustained in the daily and weekly practice of the school community, as teachers plan and work together in their own departments, consciously implementing the changes that they committed to making.

Practitioner-based professional development drives the work. Professional development is led by experienced teachers who are still primarily in the classroom, so participants are able to see examples from practitioners who do (in real schools, with real kids) what they aspire to do. Teachers want more than just reading about or seeing a presentation about a particular approach. They want hands-on workshops where teachers experience the method firsthand—where they tackle open-ended math problems, experience responsive Spanish instruction, grapple with texts, and reflect on their experience as learners.

Additionally, teachers must spend substantial time working collaboratively to develop lesson plans and assessments to bring back to their sites, and share these lessons, assessments, and student work with each other in structured sessions. Groups learn from their peers, not just from an "expert" in the room.

Teachers learn structures to make collaboration productive. The use of protocols greatly enhances the work of collaborative groups in several ways. First, the teacher presenting the work articulates the kind of critical feedback they seek. Then, the group has clear supports and structures to keep the conversation focused and moving forward, with an eye toward making the most of the limited time they have together.

Guidelines for participation (both for when and how to contribute, and when to listen) help balance the voices at the table and increase the range of perspectives and contributions. Finally, the reflective closing at the end of each protocol invites all participants, not just the presenter, to consider how the work influences their own professional practice. In these conversations, teachers examine student work samples to align their expectations for quality work, fine-tune assessment tasks and lesson plans, and problem-solve issues of implementation that inevitably arise in the midst of change.

School leaders create conditions where teachers and students can take risks. Clear communication with the entire school community about a common vision of what student-centered learning will look like helps everyone understand and work toward a common goal. Making time for teachers to collaborate with each other strengthens the work. Buffering, where possible, some of the many competing demands experienced in a school helps sustain a focus on what is really important.

Teachers have access to resources, models, and support. Coaching support is built into the school year annually. Additional professional development and coaching are brought in as teachers request help, and the sessions are designed to tackle the questions teachers most want to address. Many schools still use textbooks as a major resource in classes. *Teachers need resources beyond the text, as well as a green light to view the text as a resource, not the curriculum.* Teachers do not have to re-create the wheel in each individual school, but can, through their expanded professional network, find resources to help them design high-quality, student-centered instruction.

FINAL REFLECTIONS

Moving toward a culture of inquiry requires time and patience. Schools that were able to make significant progress focused on (1) creating a culture of inquiry centered on meeting the unique needs of their students; (2) helping teachers develop inquiry teaching and assessment practices in the classroom; (3) developing collaborative structures among teachers that enabled them to use a cycle of inquiry to explore meaningful questions about real problems of practice; and (4) working with school leaders to understand the guiding principles for the work and craft a vision and action plan for their schools. These four areas can serve as entry points for any school or district to begin the work of shifting toward a culture of inquiry.

Schools that successfully transform into inquiry-based learning environments reap many benefits. Successful schools see a marked increase in the levels and types of student engagement. Because much of the learning is driven by student interest and exploration, students inevitably develop a sense of self-efficacy and new attitudes about the classroom. Schools also saw a marked increase in the quality and depth of teacher collaboration.

NOTES

1. *Inquiry-Based Learning*, Pittsfield Middle High School video, http://www.pittsfieldnhschools.org.
2. http://i3.cssr.us/culture-of-inquiry.

Chapter Three

The Power of Network

"Scientists have power by virtue of the respect commanded by the discipline. . . . We live with poets and politicians, preachers and philosophers. All have their ways of knowing, and all are valid in their proper domain. The world is too complex and interesting for one way to hold all the answers."— Stephen Jay Gould, *Bully for Brontosaurus: Reflections in Natural History*

Making the transformational shift toward student-driven learning requires intentional design choices to harness the power of networking both within and across schools. How does a school develop a community of learners through the power of a network in order to create the conditions that build capacity among stakeholders and support the structures for effective implementation for sustainability and culture change?

The value of peer-to-peer collaboration that includes varied viewpoints builds capacity by supporting the school change process. The Springdale, Arkansas, school district (the second largest in the state) is a very innovative district that has benefited greatly from its involvement in the network of districts that regularly support each other through the Race to the Top district networking opportunities. All the districts have been able to vet personalized student-centered learning across a group of districts wrestling with similar challenges.

Similarly, the Secondary School Network, organized and conducted by Brown University between 1996 and 2006, provided strong networking opportunities for secondary schools across the northeast that led to major changes in school, district, and state policy and practice across the New England states. Additionally, the National High School Alliance, a network of more than forty organizations, regularly came together to exchange ideas on high school redesign that provided the basis for a *Call to Action*, a groundbreaking new look at the challenges addressed in changing high schools to provide for the varying needs of each and every student.

The New England Network for Personalization and Performance (NENPP) provides a proven model of how a network could be organized to provide real value for each network member. NENPP includes thirteen high schools in eleven districts across four states. The examples in this chapter are drawn from the specific experience of the NENPP network, but the examples offered here can apply to any network of schools or districts.

Changing school culture requires questioning the traditional philosophy of "my kids, my classroom." For far too long, educators have operated within the confines of their four classroom walls in what one site coordinator called "pure isolation." In order to make the transformational shift toward "whole school community" learning, NENPP made intentional design choices to harness the power of networking, and employed skilled facilitative leadership to support each site in accomplishing grant goals.

Through a collaborative process and multiple learning opportunities for teachers, students, and school administrators, schools were able to move out of isolation and better understand the possibilities of inquiry-based instruction and other best practices. The NENPP team created opportunities for individual school-based site teams to develop strategies and support structures to examine their own professional development through reflection, refinement, and skill building. Over time, site teams became the drivers of change where stakeholders felt comfortable taking risks and trying new strategies.

> "It is really nice to see what other schools are doing and to learn from our school change coaches who always came in with an eye towards development and change. I highly encourage more schools to engage in the networking process because it is comforting to know I can pick up the phone and call a colleague in another state and say we are struggling with something—how did you guys do it? That outside lens would help us when we felt like we were getting caught up not being able to see the forest through the trees. The conversation would just help us see things differently."—Peggy Reynolds, site coordinator, Nashua High School North and South

The NENPP created the following network components to reap the benefits of networking:

Performance Assessment Working Group (PAWG). A group of teacher leaders from each school met monthly to look collaboratively at student work across the NENPP. This involved sharing and improving lessons and assessments, scoring student work, and reviewing teacher-developed units against a clear outside standard. Students became increasingly involved in this work over time—they not only attended PAWG meetings to lend their voice to instructional practices, but they also presented work created in collaboration with teachers.

Performance Assessment Review (PAR) Board. This group, led and facilitated by outside experts and practitioners, made multiday school visits to each NENPP school on two occasions over the project period. Members of school site visiting teams provided focused feedback to the schools on how to create lasting change for each school in its specific school community.

Summer Institute. This annual multiday event brought together representatives from all stakeholder groups (students, teachers, administrators, and community members) for an opportunity to network and learn together. Participants presented summaries of their work in structured, small groups—in order to both celebrate their successes and solicit critical feedback for improvement.

School Coaching. A cadre of highly experienced school change coaches worked collaboratively in each school setting. They continuously analyzed school needs and responded by designing work locally to be carried out with the expertise of the coaching team. Coaches acted as facilitators helping schools ask the right questions and see learning and teaching from a different point of view.

The networking components outlined above, and described later in more detail, would not have been possible without two critical components: planning and facilitation. The embedded structures within each school building, and across the entire thirteen-school network, allowed for collaboration and risk taking to be the norm. With courage and a commitment to individual and team skill-building, powerful networks flourished and dramatically impacted the overall success of the NENPP project.

NETWORK PLANNING

In planning for powerful networks within the i3 project, the Center for Secondary School Redesign (CSSR) committed to the following design elements for each networking component:

Purpose—why the specific networking component was a key element

Membership—who would be involved in this aspect of networking

Value—benefit to the members

Inclusion—how all stakeholders, specifically students, could be meaningfully engaged in the work

Operating principles—how the group would function and the goals on which it would focus

Coordination, facilitation, and communication within each network subgroup—who would organize, communicate, and facilitate the work

Continuous improvement—use of reflection and evaluation to continually assess and adjust the work

An intentional effort was made to design networking components to support the work of all stakeholders, including students, classroom teachers, and school leaders. A collaborative team planned for each networking component, as well as evaluated, responded to, and adjusted each networking component, at least annually, with an eye to improvement and refinement of the work.

Commitment to the networking components of the i3 project intensified over time and gained power as relationships developed. Powerful networking created checks and balances that mitigated individual biases and allowed the impact of the network to grow by leaps and bounds over time. This formal collaboration, what CSSR calls a high-performing team, served as the true engine for change.

Support for the demonstration of courage is essential when initiating major school change and transformation, allowing the creativity and innovation from the team to drive all future activities, tasks, and practices. This approach modeled the behavior and practices CSSR encourages school leaders to embrace in shifting away from a traditional teacher-centered culture, to a more student-driven inquiry-based culture.

NETWORK FACILITATION

Successful facilitation of high-performing-team conversation is required. Skilled facilitative leadership is essential for expanding the power of a network. Successful facilitation actively engages team members to leverage everyone's talents and contributions and build consensus.

Effective facilitative leadership involves using processes and tools to maximize the individual and collective intelligence of the team to determine the right course of action and act on the choices they make. This includes making it easy for others to offer their unique perspectives and talents, speaking up when they have problems, taking the initiative, making appropriate decisions, working with others, and sharing responsibility for the accomplishments of the group. Skilled facilitative leaders build the capacity of both the individuals and the group in the following ways:

- Make connections and help others build meaning through purposeful conversation
- Balance content with a process that brings the groups expertise
- Regularly reflect on progress and purpose
- Provide direction to enable the group to articulate its own next steps
- Act transparently to invite productive feedback

• Ensure that everyone understands and agrees to the purpose of the team

Planning for powerful networks, including the use of skilled facilitative leadership, is critical to replicating the success of the NENPP project in new places. The intentionally collaborative design of the networking components is vital to allowing the time, structure, and support needed for projects to flourish. In the following sections, each providing a detailed overview of the networking components of the NENPP project, evidence of the planning and facilitation of each component is included.

PERFORMANCE ASSESSMENT WORKING GROUP

The Performance Assessment Working Group (PAWG) was a group of teacher leaders from each school who met monthly to look collaboratively at student work across the NENPP. This involved sharing and improving lessons and assessments, scoring student work, and reviewing teacher-developed units against a clear outside standard. Students became increasingly involved in this work over time—not only attending PAWG meetings to lend their voice to instructional practices, but also presenting work created in collaboration with teachers.

PAWG was a highly successful networking component, created in direct response to the grant's goal of strengthening authentic assessment practices throughout the NENPP. The purpose of PAWG was to gather a group of practitioners from each school to look collaboratively at student work and learn how to effectively assess the work of students and teachers. PAWG evolved in response to the changing needs and growing capacities of the participating schools.

PAWG consisted of a variable group of representatives of the thirteen schools who met monthly to review artifacts of performance assessment and progress toward transformational, student-driven, inquiry-based learning environments. PAWG met at a different school each month, and CSSR coaches initially facilitated meetings.

Before each PAWG meeting, CSSR coaches assisted the PAWG representative of the host school in preparing an agenda that pinpointed what student and teacher work would be examined and which protocols were best suited to provide the presenter with the most useful feedback (see figure 3.1). The most commonly used protocols in PAWG work were tuning, validation, and moderation/calibration protocols.

The agenda also included an opening activity and a review of the norms of the group. The host school usually highlighted an ongoing project, plan, or dilemma such as site council, senior project, or extended learning opportunities (ELOs). This provided deep learning for both the visitors and the host

PAWG Protocols

    Step 1 - Introduction (5 minutes) Facilitator briefly introduces protocol goals, guidelines, and schedule

    Step 2 - Presentation (10-15 minutes) The presenter has the opportunity to share both the context for her work and any supporting documents as warranted, while participants are silent. Presenter provides:

- Information about the students and/or the class — what the students tend to be like, where they are in school, where they are in the year.
- Assignment or prompt that generated the student work
- Student learning goals or standards that inform the work
- Samples of student work — photocopies of work, video clips, etc. — with student names removed
- Evaluation format — scoring rubric and or assessment criteria, etc.
- Focusing question for feedback (ex: To what extent does the student work reflect the learning standards? Or, How might the rubric be in closer alignment to the skills and knowledge present in the student work?) is shared and posted for all to see.

    Step 3 - Clarifying Questions (3-5 minutes) Participants have an opportunity to ask clarifying questions in order to get information that may have been omitted during the presentation and would help them to better understand the work.

- Clarifying questions are matters of fact.
- The facilitator is responsible for making sure that clarifying questions are really clarifying and not warm/cool feedback or suggestions.

    Step 4 - Examining the Work (10-15 minutes) Participants look closely at the work, making notes on where it seems to be "in tune" or aligned with the stated goals and, guided by the presenter's focusing question and goals, where there might be a potential disconnect.

    Step 5 - Pause to Silently Reflect on Warm and Cool Feedback (2-3 minutes) Participants individually review their notes and decide what they would like to contribute to the feedback session. The Presenter is silent and participants do this work silently.

    Step 6 - Warm and Cool Feedback (10-15 minutes) Participants share feedback with each other while the presenter is silent and takes notes. The feedback generally begins with a few minutes of warm feedback, moves on to a few minutes of cool feedback (sometimes phrased in the form of reflective questions), and then moves back and forth between warm and cool feedback.

    S*tep 7 - Reflection* (3-5 minutes) The Presenter rejoins the group and shares her/his new thinking about what she/he learned from the participants' feedback.

- This is not a time for the presenter to defend her/himself, but is instead a time for the presenter to reflect aloud on anything that seemed particularly interesting.

Figure 3.1. Performance Assessment Working Group protocols.

school and was a significant means of moving them forward across the network.

The PAWG work began slowly and gained momentum rapidly. It took time for members to become familiar with the tools and processes for looking collaboratively at student work. Over time, the group learned how to effectively present their work to the other group members, how to participate by giving targeted feedback, and how to facilitate a productive conversation about important aspects of teaching and learning using structured conversations and formal protocols.

As a result, PAWG members were instrumental in bringing *collaborative practices trainings* to their own schools. A dynamic synergy developed between the PAWG and collaborative practices segments of the NENPP program. As PAWG members deepened their skills, they began leading the facilitation of monthly meetings. By encouraging colleagues at their schools to get trained, they supported the creation of school-based groups that engaged regularly in authentic assessment practices such as tuning student and adult work, validation, moderation, and data analysis.

The outcome for PAWG members engaged in this work was twofold: members developed a deep understanding of performance assessments and how to use them on a regular basis to improve student learning; they also gained experience using structured protocols for collaboration. The development of facilitation skills on the part of all PAWG members was a key element of sustaining the work at their schools and encouraging meaningful professional collaboration among their colleagues. Over time, PAWG members took over from the CSSR coach the role of facilitation. Additionally, districts increasingly included students in their delegations.

By the fourth year of working together, PAWG developed a five-point scale to measure how far NENPP schools had come along the path to using the power of a network to implement performance assessments as part of a transformational, student-driven, inquiry-based culture:

Stage 1—majority of teachers work in isolation

Stage 2—some teachers/departments have built capacity to discuss, give feedback, and look at student work collaboratively

Stage 3—most departments have capacity to look at student work; teachers routinely tune adult and student work; some students are involved

Stage 4—calibration and validation take place in most departments; increasing number of students are involved

Stage 5—calibration and validation are now the norm; students are routinely engaged

All NENPP schools moved purposefully along this continuum at their own pace. Each school embraced the concepts, but the implementation was personalized to meet the needs of their unique stakeholders. Over the five years that the network has been collaborating, all NENPP schools had attained stage 3 and many had moved beyond into stages 4 and 5. Two key elements were critical to the success and impact of the PAWG group:

Transparent facilitation. The CSSR coaches, and later the PAWG members themselves, were responsive to cues from the group—changing and adapting protocols to fit the circumstances and deepen the learning. In time, all members became skillful facilitators capable of leading a protocol and planning suitable activities.

Involving students. As schools gained confidence, they increasingly saw the power of having students at the table for these rich and meaningful conversations about practice. Increasingly students became involved in PAWG meetings, particularly when PAWG visited their school. Some of the most significant learning from PAWG sessions took place when students led the way.

PAWG made a significant contribution to advancing the goals of the NENPP and ensuring the sustainability of the work. The PAWG work gave teachers the confidence to feel good about what they were doing in the classroom and with their colleagues. Several sites are initiating local district-wide K–12 PAWGs as a result of their involvement in the NENPP.

"What I was doing was a good thing and I was not the outsider by focusing on the kids because we all were bringing the same energy each month and then bringing it back home to share with our teachers and students. The incredible thing was that the experience brought together teachers from different content areas. You were looking at the work and improving your practice through sharing, and reflection. It was an eye opener for me."—PAWG member

PERFORMANCE ASSESSMENT REVIEW (PAR) BOARD

Early in the development of the NENPP it was recognized that the work would benefit by having a broad-based group of educators, policy makers, and community members to advise on the practices, procedures, and guidelines to be used in giving feedback on the work completed within the thirteen high schools. The Performance Assessment Review (PAR) Board was modeled after the work done by the New York Performance Standards Consortium and structured in a way that would deliver value to the unique NENPP. Based on the suggestion of our original PAR Board chair, Dr. Melissa Roderick from the University of Chicago, PAR Board school site visit members included not only outside experts and stakeholders, but internal teachers, students, and administrators from within the NENPP schools. This approach cultivated a powerful network of learners and allowed for a collaborative implementation of the innovative i3 strategies.

The PAR Board consisted of twenty members representing higher education, practicing educators, policy makers, and recipients of previous grants.

The diverse backgrounds of the PAR Board membership promoted creative thinking and resulted in nuanced, insightful feedback for the schools. The PAR Board modeled the collegial networking that was sought from the thirteen member schools by using an inquiry model based on CSSR best practices for *personalizing for performance*. This included a common set of assessment measures, but an uncommon set of tasks to support progress toward project outcomes.

Over a five-year period, the PAR Board conducted two site visits at each NENPP school. Site visit teams included three PAR Board members and representatives from each network school—including students. A set of site visit activities were developed to bring structure to the visit for site visitors, school personnel, and students. The PAR Board site visit process included the following critical tasks:

- PAR Board facilitation teams consisting of two to three experts planned and prepared the two-day visits with the host school leaders and CSSR coaches.
- The PAR Board visit leader finalized the agenda, outcomes, and grant alignment activities with the host school.
- The two-day visit was open to outside school visitors.
- The PAR Board team conducted a debrief discussion with school staff and students to identify key findings and suggestions to be outlined in the site visit report.
- The final draft of the site visit report was vetted with the visiting team and host school leadership.

PAR Board site visits reaffirmed the successes schools demonstrated in meeting grant objectives and offered guidance for next steps. Visits included introduction and orientation on the first day; student participation via representative teams from other NENPP schools; students leading open discussions; and single students completing their work on extended learning opportunities (ELOs). Classroom visits focused on new initiatives and meetings with classroom practitioners in the form of collaborative practice sessions focused on tuning work or problem solving current dilemmas.

At the conclusion of each site visit, the site visit leader facilitated a debrief session with PAR Board members and visitors from across the other NENPP schools. The debrief session was also open to other stakeholders (educators, students, community members) from the host school. The PAR Board gathered feedback from the site visit, including the interactive debrief session, to produce a site visit report that included observations, findings, and suggestions. In many of the schools, the CSSR coaches facilitated a text-based reading of the report with the full faculty in order to establish an action plan for the remaining years of the grant.

The second site visit (which took place two years later) became a way to gauge to what extent sites had been successful in meeting the issues raised during the first site visit. As an example, one district used its District Site Committee to analyze the first report, which underscored the absence of genuine student voices and the domince of adult voices. With the guidance of their CSSR school change coach, they agreed to protocols that ensured the equal presence of all voices.

By year five of the network, all thirteen schools were demonstrating progress as a direct result of powerful networking through the PAR Board. The PAR Board members quickly learned that collegial dialogue enabled relationship building and emergence of trust between and among stakeholders. Visits became increasingly influential once schools understood that site visitors were focused on offering validation, guidance, and recommendations, rather than criticism about that which had not yet been accomplished. A highlight of the PAR Board work was the impact on students. Recommendations from site visits influenced broader policy and practices that directly impacted the entire student population. As a result, students had the opportunity for genuine leadership experiences within the larger learning community.

Students like Kellie, a junior from Nashua, had the opportunity to engage in the PAR Board process and create an authentic learning opportunity through an ELO based on her networking with other school leaders. "An ELO lets you explore your own personal interests and dictate your own educational experience; you are in charge of it. What struck me right off the bat at my first PAR visit was the lack of student presence. This is what gave me the idea to make an ELO about student voice and achievement. The opportunity to learn from others and see what goes into this type of change was incredible," said Kellie.

SUMMER INSTITUTE

The Summer Institute, a multiday symposium providing targeted support and multiple learning opportunities, was the incubator for innovative strategy sharing and refinement of inquiry-based learning strategies within the NENPP project. Each year the institute accommodated around 160 total participants including students, teachers, and administrators. The institute was a powerful networking opportunity for building relationships and alliances across schools that were mutually beneficial to building capacity and sustaining the project goals and outcomes well beyond the five years of the grant. Like nearly all other aspects of the NENPP, the Summer Institute grew in both substance and influence over time. As the content of each school's work grew in import, the opportunity for networking followed the same trajectory.

"Each summer the conversation was very different and was focused on the key elements of building skills over time so that capacity was in place to sustain the changes well after the grant ended."—Janet Allison, former executive director of the New England Association of Schools and Colleges (NEASC) and PAR Board member

CSSR used the Summer Institute as an opportunity to increase stakeholder proficiency and effort strategically over the five-year project. The institute was structured to answer the following three guiding questions:

- What capabilities do I as an NENPP stakeholder need to be successful?
- What is my current level of proficiency to meet the goals and outcomes of the grant with fidelity, and change classroom culture?
- How do I continue to become more proficient over time and improve my practice?

As reflected in the snippets below, each Summer Institute followed the stages of knowledge, skill, and talent acquisition.

Year 1 (Stage 1): Find Value in Work Based on Understanding

The first Summer Institute was led and directed by CSSR coaches to explore the vision and possibilities for the i3 work. Reviewing the NENPP initiatives and outcomes was only of value once participants better understood where they were going, and why. Participants were prepared to engage in conversation based on their learning from a text-based conversation on the value of authentic pedagogy. Time and coaching support (conditions for success) were provided for school teams to meet and chart their work for the coming school year. The action plans created during these team-planning opportunities became the foundations of planning for year 2 of implementation.

Year 2 (Stages 2 and 3): Recognize Areas for Personal and Professional Growth

The second Summer Institute began the shift away from the "*what*" of inquiry-based learning (i.e., What is inquiry-based learning? What does inquiry-based learning look like in my classroom?) to the "*how*" of inquiry-based learning (How do I change my mental models to engage in student-driven learning experiences in the classroom?). Participants completed a self-assessment and evaluated their actions and behaviors in order to recognize areas of personal and professional development that they and their colleagues must go through to embrace an inquiry-based approach.

Based on the coaching done in project year 1, the institute provided targeted professional development opportunities using a seminar model where participants self-selected interest strands such as collaborative skills and practices; courageous conversations in school leadership; and (content-specific) inquiry and assessment strategies. Sites were required to bring students to the Summer Institute, who followed a strand on student agency.

The conversations among adults and students highlighted the need for a larger network-wide conversation examining student work and exploring inquiry-based pedagogy. These conversations, contentious at times, led to the creation of the Performance Assessment Working Group, and were an important step away from group "storming" into group "performing."

Year 3 (Stage 4): Using Calibration and Moderation to Deepen Learning Experiences

The third Summer Institute focused on developing and refining inquiry-based learning units and authentic assessment practices. Participants could be more engaged in deeper learning activities that built upon their experience in years 1 and 2. For the first time, participants completed a moderation of student work within content area teams, which asked them to present artifacts of student work that were assessed by the group using a common rubric.

Many participants were fearful and confused during the moderation study—reflective of the isolation under which many practitioners operate in their professional practice. The results of this activity set the stage for a yearlong PAWG focus on structured conversations and activities that addressed the following issues: looking at student work, calibration, validation, and moderation. The results of the initial moderation study in year 3 set the stage for one of the greatest successes in the project, the year 4 moderation study.

Year 4 (Stage 5): Refinement of the Calibration and Moderation Processes

The CSSR team planned for three major outcomes during the fourth Summer Institute: (1) conduct a calibration and validation study that *included students* at the table providing feedback on assessment of selected student work; (2) expand the work of content area teams to develop curriculum plans, assessment tools, and rubrics—using authentic work artifacts brought from their classrooms; and (3) explore leadership requirements for the final phase of the project and sustainability of the work in the future.

Schools were now ready to take the lead, and work sessions were increasingly facilitated by participants with coaches' support. Resulting from the initial poorly received moderation study in 2013, and following a yearlong focus on collaborative skills training, the fourth Summer Institute included calibration and validation activities on the final day that exceeded expectations.

Facilitated by well-trained PAWG members, and including more than thirty students from across the NENPP, participants looked collaboratively at student and teacher tasks—a process that had become routine to a majority of the participants. Students who attended the institute added their rich voices and insights to the discussions of lessons and units, and teachers were ready to embrace the feedback and adjust their practice based on what they heard.

Year 5 (Stage 6): Celebrating Success and Planning for Continuous Improvement

The fifth NENPP Summer Institute was an opportunity for schools to demonstrate proficiency as high-performing teams. Students and staff from each school were given full autonomy to share and facilitate all workshops and conversations. Conversations were structured around the following five areas: culture of inquiry, student agency, student-driven learning, the power of networks, and shared leadership and sustainability.

The second day of the institute featured a school showcase where each NENPP school presented two seventy-five-minute workshops highlighting one or two of their best practices—an opportunity to share with other practitioners the areas of school redesign of which they were most proud. The institute was focused on sustaining grant work, and the majority of sites indicated that they were preserving many project roles after year 5.

The powerful networking opportunities that took place over the five project years were the result of measured planning and contextually based adjustments. Each year expectations were raised for attendees: to work together on performance assessments; to increase their use of collaborative practices; and to include students in increasingly meaningful ways in the redesign process. Each of the five Summer Institutes began and ended with a student focus, and student involvement and influence grew as the grant work developed. More than forty students attended the 2015 Summer Institute, and in many cases, they acted as lead presenters for their school's work.

SCHOOL CHANGE COACHING

The coach role is essential to connecting the goals of any grant within the unique environment of each school. The coach is not a consultant but instead someone with a very unique skill set who is able to cultivate relationships over time, and uses a plethora of tools and strategies to organically build knowledge from within. Responsive coaching is a balancing act and includes a comprehensive approach to addressing instruction, leadership, and culture change.

To be successful, school coaches must work hand in hand with school staff—in order to help them envision what is now possible and build their capacity for influencing both heart and mind. With a coach's guidance, the building stakeholders become the experts over time. CSSR school change coaches played a critical role in guiding the establishment and sustainability of the powerful networks created through the i3 project.

An effective coach accepts ambiguity and works with the school based on where they are now and can possibly go in the future—coaches take a philosophical stance to culture change that says "go slow to go fast." Coaching in the NENPP varied considerably according to each school's culture and the depth of its commitment to fundamental change. The coaches provided support for, and modeling of, the shift away from traditional teacher-centered instruction and test-based assessment, to instruction centered on student work and assessment based on the meaningful application of essential knowledge and skills.

To be successful this shift requires personalizing the school environment by empowering students to collaborate in making school policy, and partnering with faculty and administration in fundamental choices related to how and what they learn.

The CSSR approach to coaching is team driven and embraces the power of a community of learners. Over the five-year project, CSSR school change coaches were flexible in providing coaching support that best met the needs of participating sites. Initially, two coaches worked together at each school. One coach focused on the *change culture team*, composed largely of the principal and school leaders and charged with promoting the personalization of the school environment. The second coach focused on the *authentic assessment team*, composed mostly of teachers and students and charged with supporting the shift to inquiry-based learning and performance-based assessment.

As sites' needs changed over time, coach roles did as well. In the final years of the grant, coaches focused on three specific areas of practice: *student voice and choice, collaborative practices*, and *inquiry-based instruction*. Nearly all NENPP schools have taken advantage of these coaching services to offer successful professional development programs—furthering school goals and ensuring sustainability of the work.

Coaching works best when coaches and school stakeholders collaborate and support each other's work; take time to understand one another and integrate into the school environment; and build lasting capacity into the work of students, teachers, and administrators so that high school can be a place where learning can happen anytime, anyplace, any pace.

"I discovered after 40 years in the work that we could assemble a network of regular schools in order to begin to address some of the issues that they faced, with some of the potential that we could bring in terms of facilitation and co-creation. We partnered with people to talk about what their issues are and helped them find their own solutions with the skills and knowledge and understanding that coaches brought to the table. At the end of the [2014] Summer Institute I thought 'where I am right now in this group and this time is what I've been dreaming of doing my entire professional life' because I didn't think it was possible. Now I know it's possible."—Dr. Gregg Sinner, CSSR school change coach

FINAL REFLECTIONS

The power of networking in the NENPP was transformational for the individuals and schools involved. Sites modeled collaborative learning, deepened relationships, fostered the cross-pollination of ideas, and confronted seemingly intractable barriers to systemic and sustainable change, which unleashed multiplier effects within and across the thirteen participating schools.

Participants used the networking opportunities to engage in deep conversations based on pedagogy, student needs, and the role we all play in changing school culture. Strong facilitation allowed all voices to be heard and for participants to better understand how the project, the coaching, and the best practices were changing the fabric of what school is and could be.

Whereas the data suggests that the schools are demonstrating improvement in student engagement and increasing student performance as a result of the work, the real success comes from the conversations and the experiences influencing all project stakeholders to think long and hard about their own practice and the state of learning and teaching within their school building, across the NENPP, and throughout the country.

PROTOCOLS

Calibration Protocol

Purpose: To calibrate the scoring of student work and explore instructional implications.

Materials and Timeframe: An individual teacher or a group of teachers assigns a task and assessment. They bring three samples of the resulting student work and the evaluation they will use for the group. Each participant should have a packet containing the three exemplars of typical student work along with the rubric/checklist or evaluation tool evaluation. Approximately 65 minutes.

Process

Step 1—The facilitator reviews and walks the group through the calibration process as outlined in the protocol (2 minutes).

Step 2—The teacher passes out the work and shares the context briefly (3 minutes).

Step 3—In silence, the participants examine the materials (5 minutes).

Step 4—The group asks clarifying questions about the materials and process (5 minutes).

Step 5—Working in silence, the participants independently read and annotate three student work samples noting evidence of meeting the standard. Participants record their observations, making notes. The presenter can participate (15 minutes).

Step 6—The facilitator invites each member to share his or her annotations and observations of the work referring to evidence in the student work. Group members listen as each participant shares their work. Notes are charted, but there is no discussion (15 minutes).

Step 7—Each member uses the evaluation provided to score the three work samples. Members individually share their scores, and a group scoring chart is created (10 minutes).

Step 8—The group looks at where consensus exists on scoring and discusses difference in scoring and if consensus can be reached (10 minutes).

Step 9—Debrief the activity by discussing each of the questions below:

- What did we notice about scoring the student work and checklist?
- What might be the next steps for supporting the work of these students?
- How might the teacher improve the assigned task, prompt, and instructions?
- What are the implications for our practice as teachers? (10 minutes)

Step 10—Thank the participants for their work.

Validation Protocol

Purpose: The validation protocol has been developed to analyze teacher-developed units of study against a clear set of outside standards. The protocol provides presenters with focused, detailed feedback on their work, which can be used for revision. Additionally, work that reaches high standards can be shared with other teachers and among networks of schools. The activity takes roughly 60 minutes to complete.

Process

Step 1—Facilitator sets the stage (5 minutes) and reviews the task and protocol.

Step 2—Presenter shares the task/assignment and the context for the work followed by clarifying questions being asked and answered (5 minutes); clarifying questions are matters of fact.

Step 3—*Examination of the Task / Assessment* (5 minutes): Participants review the task / assessment, and additional clarifying questions are asked and answered as needed.

Step 4—Presenter leaves the group (15 minutes): Participants complete a validation checklist individually, and participants prepare feedback individually by making written notes.

Step 5—*Validation Review:* Participants share each section of the validation checklist, discussing the following questions and seeking consensus on the task/assessment. Participants discuss feedback and questions, which would be useful to the presenting teacher (15 minutes).

5A. Alignment: Is the task, assignment, or assessment aligned to . . . specific content standards and (or intended parts of content standards and are twenty-first-century skills addressed by including multiple modalities (if appropriate)?

5B. Depth of Knowledge (DOK) Levels: Are the DOK levels appropriate for the task?

Depth of Knowledge (DOK) Level Descriptions

DOK 1: Includes recall; memorization; simple understanding of a word or phrase.

DOK 2: Covers level 1 plus: paraphrase; summarize; interpret; infer; classify; organize; compare; and determine fact from fiction.

DOK 3: Students must support their thinking by citing references from text or other sources. Students are asked to go beyond the text to analyze, generalize, or connect ideas. Requires deeper knowledge. Items may require abstract reasoning, inferences between and across readings, application of prior knowledge, or text support for an analytical judgment about a text.

DOK 4: Requires higher-order thinking, including complex reasoning, planning, and developing of concepts. Usually applies to an extended task or project. Examples: evaluates several works by the same author; critiques an issue across time periods or researches topic/issue from different perspectives; longer investigations or research projects.

5C. Quality of Task Design: Does the task, assignment, or assessment focus on what is intended to be demonstrated—will the assessment highlight what the student knows and can do related to the chosen standards and benchmarks?

5D. Clarity and Focus: Does the task, assignment, or assessment address an essential issue, big idea, or key concept or skill of the unit/course? Does the task clearly indicate what the student is being asked to do?

5E. Student Engagement: Does the task, assignment, or assessment provide for student ownership and decision making, requiring the student to be actively engaged, including authentic problems and issues generated by student interest?

5F. Fairness: Is the task, assignment, or assessment fair and unbiased in language and design with material familiar to students from identifiable cultural, gender, linguistic, and other groups? Is it free of stereotypes? Do all students have access to needed resources? And does the task, assignment, or assessment allow for accommodations for students with specific learning plans?

5G. Adherence to Principles of Universal Design: Instructions are free of wordiness and irrelevant information and free of unusual words students may not understand. Does the format clearly indicate what the actual questions and prompts are?

5H. Criteria and Levels: Do rubric(s) or scoring guide(s) assess all intended parts of content standards?

Step 6—Feedback: Presenter returns to the group. Participants share their feedback on the work. It is helpful to begin with "warm feedback" (what seems to be in alignment) and then move to "cool feedback" (wonderings and probing questions) (10 minutes).

Step 7—Debrief: The facilitator leads a debrief. The group then discusses how the protocol may have affected their own practice and its usefulness as a tool for developing fair and effective assignments and assessment.

Chapter Four

Shared Leadership

"If you've got students' interests at your core and all of your efforts are designed to move students forward, you're not going to go too far wrong. You may need to adjust your course a bit but if that's what's driving you, if that's what's pulling you forward, you're going to be okay."—Peggy Reynolds, director of secondary curriculum, Nashua High Schools

Shared leadership is especially important in high-demand environments like schools. Creating leadership "density"—beyond those in "positional" authority—can greatly accelerate the change process.

When we think of leaders, we typically imagine an individual or individuals who are positioned at the top of a hierarchy—or "positional leaders." This traditional definition of leadership exists in most organizations, and effective "positional" leadership is, indeed, critical to school change. The complexity of change in schools requires that we recognize a broader definition of leadership that is shared and distributed across a wide array of stakeholders—including students. What we learned time and again is that leadership can pop up in the most surprising places in an organization and that leadership "density" can greatly accelerate the change process.

In New England Network for Personalization and Performance (NENPP) schools, exemplary leadership emerged in teachers, site coordinators, administrators, students, parents, and community members. Having leaders across the organization and community is perhaps the most effective way, if not the only way, of ensuring that change will "stick" because many individuals own it. Shared leadership focuses on fostering communication, cooperation, and collaboration in an organization; it is built on a commitment to realizing both individual and organizational goals.

Shared leadership is especially important in high-demand environments like a high school, in which there are many moving parts and in which all of

47

those parts are interconnected in some way. Distributing the leadership across the organization will likely require a level of sophistication and proficiency that has not previously been expected of those who work in schools. Creating a student-driven environment requires that new leadership skills be developed across the organization. In essence, shared leadership changes the culture—the values, norms, and deeply held beliefs that are beneath the surface of day-to-day behavior. The following core elements of shared leadership serve as the enabler to authentic culture change:

Students. Students are fully engaged in school change and viewed as partners in the redesign process—having a role on most leadership teams.

Compelling vision. All stakeholders are working in unison toward common and innovative student outcomes.

Collaboration. Formal mechanisms are in place to provide the entire school community with regular opportunities for structured collaboration.

Influence and energy. School leaders prioritize initiatives and best practices in a way that structures energy and influence toward the activities that have the greatest impact on student achievement.

Capacity building. Teachers, students, and administrators are not only focusing on tangible classroom practices, but also cultivating the intrinsic behaviors that will sustain change and continue to develop relationships and build trust over time.

Developing shared leadership must be responsive to those people who say "I can't." What they may really be saying is "I am afraid to, or don't know how to or both." Those who say "I don't want to" present a different challenge. Developing leadership skills among stakeholders happens over time—not through one or two workshops or trainings. It requires a belief in an adaptive philosophy and an ability to mobilize people to meet a set of goals and embrace a set of challenges. Figure 4.1 shows how tending to the little habits, routines, practices and processes, and systems of student-driven learning builds people's sense of efficacy, and can spark significant changes in the school culture.

Simply designating individuals as leaders, without directed professional development to give them the tools and authority necessary to act on their own, will do nothing but create resentment and chaos.

TITE THINKING

Bill Bryan, Ph.D., vice president for leadership and organizational development at the Center for Secondary School Redesign (CSSR), says that transformative leadership is all about the "human factor." That is, effective leadership throughout any learning environment is about the ability to influence and manage one's energy in a way that enhances learning to benefit student

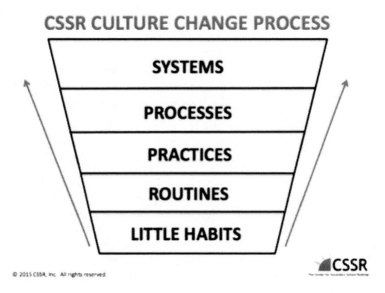

CSSR CULTURE CHANGE PROCESS

SYSTEMS

PROCESSES

PRACTICES

ROUTINES

LITTLE HABITS

CSSR

Figure 4.1. CSSR culture change process.

achievement. As part of the culture change process, positional and organic leaders take colleagues and their peers from a current state (where they are accustomed to being) to a place that is very new. In the process, leaders must create conditions that allow stakeholders to reorient themselves to embrace the emerging new culture and climate.

With a clear vision of what is possible, the journey includes helping students and teachers develop the knowledge, skills, talents, and abilities to get to where they need to be—getting comfortable working in a student-driven learning environment. CSSR provides coaching, expertise, and myriad opportunities for all the schools that we work with to embrace the "human factor." They learn to master what Bryan calls "TITE" thinking:

Thinking influence. Helping examine their habits and routines, and creating a framework for what must be done on a regular basis to change the thoughts, feelings, and behaviors of self as well as those of others.

Thinking energy. Helping leaders understand how their habits and routines, when put into practice, influence the culture as a whole and create a purposeful system of implementation. Effectiveness relies on the leader and his/her teams' ability to manage how their level of energy is used to allocate leadership responsibilities so that energy doesn't become depleted and/or wasted over time.

John Kotter, of the Harvard Business School, suggests that the "central issue at first is never strategy, structure, culture or systems. The core of the matter is always about changing the behavior of people."[1] Not to discredit alignment of strategy and structure for long-term sustainability, it is understood that successful school redesign begins with relationship and trust building. Further, it is also understood that each school needs a level of autonomy allowing it to move at its own pace and implement strategies in a way that would meet their own unique school community needs. It is important to note that the strategies below can look very different in each learning environment and evolve over time.

CULTURE CHANGE AND "BIG HITTERS"

Leadership and infrastructure capacity building are required to support significant school culture change. Leaders are primarily responsible for how student-driven best practices are to be successfully implemented. The following best practices provide stakeholders with a general roadmap for capacity building and support the design, development, implementation, and sustainability of the school redesign process. The specific context of each school requires flexibility—in order to customize school change.

The discipline of culture change. Change requires discipline that includes both values and specific skills. The three most essential values are respect, collaboration, and ethical behavior because they shape an environment where trust prevails and stakeholders fully invest in the change goals. *It is important to assume a stance of active listening.*

Focusing and optimizing what is most important. Schools usually have a multitude of demands and initiatives, leading to "initiative fatigue." It is essential to understand what initiatives will produce the best results, and then focus resources on doing those few things very well. *All stakeholders, including students, should be part of the conversation about priorities.*

Communication and buy-in. It is a rule of thumb that if a project is not encountering resistance it is not changing anything! Therefore, leaders must continuously communicate effectively for influence, not just to transmit information. Conversations across the school unearth an understanding of stakeholder need and resistance; they reveal the communication work that needs to be done. Without clear and ongoing support of the majority of stakeholders, the work does not endure.

Team development. Strong teams are *essential* to drive and sustain change initiatives. Teams engender buy-in and provide the supporting structure for the courage to make tough decisions and stick with them. Teams are the incubators for change! *It's important to set aside the time for team development; it simply doesn't happen on its own.*

Purposeful staff and professional development. It's been our experience that job satisfaction and productivity are based on job/role clarity. Having a clear picture of what is expected, along with the skills, knowledge, and abilities to implement one's role with fidelity, will optimize performance. This applies to both one's individual role within an organization, as well as to the role of teams within an organization.

Any new practice requires that agents implementing it are often required to develop new and enhanced skills to be successful. Over time, the development of a professional learning community becomes a game changer, as leaders learn to reflect, refine, and revise. Just as students must keep learning, so must all other stakeholders in a school.

FROM BEST PRACTICE TO IMPLEMENTATION STRATEGIES

A number of activities are particularly effective at planting the seeds of change, which provide the focus, momentum, and the mechanisms that drive transformation, as shown in the following sections.

Exploring the Possibilities through Site Visits and Classroom Observations

It's easy for school leaders to get caught up in the day-to-day details of running a school or classroom. As a result, they may not be able to see the forest through the trees and may feel enervated, as opposed to energized, by their work. The mere idea of change often stokes fear, along with the mindset of "we can't do that here, with these kids." All stakeholders, including students, should be given the time and space to step back and imagine the possibilities of how a different kind of learning environment might better support student learning and development.

One effective method for helping teachers, students, and administrators dream how their school of classrooms could be different is to participate in structured school visits, conversations, and authentic learning activities so that they can fully experience the components of a student-driven learning environment. Visits to schools that are already deeply engaged in the change process stimulate and expand the visions of possibility and allow stakeholders to take from the visit what is most relevant to them. It provides the foundation for a different way of "seeing" their school and taking first steps to envision a new basic blueprint. Each school community can take learning from these visits to create their own vision of what might work in their community.

School-Generated Readiness Assessment

You can't tell people that everything they have been doing is wrong and expect them to move forward. They need to have some affirmation that they have done some really purposeful things for kids, and that their entire career has not been wasted.

In other words, changing a school or district with respect for a school's history and traditions is a more effective method for engendering change than is a "fixer" mentality. Shining a light on what *is* working creates a sense of hope for schools so that they can set priorities and create strategies and structures that both honor and build on their successes. Acknowledging and honoring current successes creates fertile ground to leverage new ideas and innovation.

In 2010, CSSR created a readiness assessment to better understand what is working purposefully and well in schools, and uncover areas for growth and improvement. The results of a readiness assessment were used in the numerous districts to create a network or district-wide professional develop-ment plan that balances school-specific best practices with practices that could be applied to the district as a whole.

The readiness assessment process revealed that the professional develop-ment opportunities that were most essential to school change were in the areas of implementing student voice and choice; collaborative skills and practices; performance assessments; and project-based experiences like ex-tended learning opportunities (ELOs) and senior projects.

Student shadowing (described in detail in chapter 2) represents a great opportunity for self-assessment of the school climate and culture. It is one thing to read what best practices look like in other schools and districts, but quite another to observe and experience the impact of policy and practices being deployed in your own schoolhouse. Student shadowing is a highly effective method for understanding the daily experience of the "customer." The shadowing experience per se creates a set of faculty/student pairs for a day, during which time the faculty member's job is to follow the designated student as he or she goes about the day—in the classroom, in the cafeteria, in the school corridors, and such. This exercise builds a deep empathy for the student experience that is otherwise unattainable.

When student shadowing takes place early in the change process, it typi-cally reveals evidence that much work remains to be done. The experience grounds constructive conversations about the need for change, and allow stakeholders to point to "live" examples of success, as well as inequities or areas for growth. It organically lays the groundwork for all of the work that follows because it's grounded in the lived reality of the daily learning and schooling environment.

For example, Chris Motika, principal of Manchester High School West, in Manchester, New Hampshire, initiated student shadowing after having seen it work well at his previous post in a different school. It turned out to be a transformative moment and a turning point. *"As students and teachers, we were amazed at how irrelevant the school day really was. No wonder people were asleep by period eight. It was an eye opener from so many perspectives. We saw that the school was not personalized; it was boring."*

Perhaps the most powerful aspect of student shadowing is the debriefing of the shadowing experience at the end of the day. At Manchester West, for example, the debriefing stimulated substantive conversation about the workings of the school and enabled the development of a plan for change.

Initiative Mapping: Assessing Capacity

Virtually every school in the country is spread too thin. Initiatives and mandates pile on over the years, and there is rarely an opportunity to step back to reflect on what's working and what's not. The goal of initiative mapping is to help key stakeholders identify, focus on, and allocate the appropriate energy and resources to those efforts—programs, initiatives, and best practices—that produce positive learning outcomes.

The activity's purpose is to identify where time, resources, and energy are currently being spent. *Initiatives* are defined here as any specific activity that is new, or reflects efforts to enhance existing processes, programs, or practices.

The initiative mapping process provides a clear snapshot of how well programs and practices are aligned toward a common purpose. It also reveals the amount of time spent on efforts that may not be delivering on their promise, which often jumpstarts a much-needed conversation about priorities.

The initiative mapping process asks school stakeholders—including students—to examine all activities/initiatives currently on their plate and question the following:

- If done well, what is the impact on student achievement?
- Is the practice high yield?
- What is the current level of performance?
- What is the current level of resistance?
- What level of energy is needed to implement the initiative?
- Is the initiative mandated by local or federal policy?
- Who "owns" the initiative's ultimate success?

After groups answer these questions, the mapping process takes place where each one is ranked, prioritized, and graded against its current level of proficiency. The findings are always eye-opening. Often there are more than a hundred initiatives that our school leaders need to manage. Schools and districts begin to better understand that they are not using their influence and energy in ways that will best benefit students. All these initiatives were implemented with the hopes that they would add value to students; however, very few are achieving the intended results. Analysis and reflection force a discussion about time, energy, and attention—enabling schools to become more focused and purposeful.

Creating High-Performing Teams

Effective teams are critical for shared leadership and an important engine for change. Ironically, most schools have too many teams, and they often function at a mediocre level at best.

There is an enormous difference between a high-performing team (HPT) and an ad hoc task team, or a team that lacks a formal structure and charter (see figures 4.2 and 4.3). HPTs are characterized by the discipline that comes with a formalized structure, policies, and procedures. By this definition, most schools do not have HPTs. Below is a sequence for creating HPTs that CSSR finds to be highly effective.

1. Create the team and develop its purpose. In many schools, there are several teams formed to lead change. For example, in the NENPP two high-performing teams were created to serve the redesign process. The change leadership team's purpose was to develop and implement key organizational processes and structures that would help support the implementation of change. Both teachers and students made up the authentic assessment team. This team was tasked to examine student-driven best practices and classroom strategies to improve learning via inquiry-based instruction and competencies.
2. Develop the infrastructure. To be truly focused on a common vision, each team requires a charter that identifies core values and actions, behaviors, and practices around which the team organizes itself. Team facilitation is important, and a set of skill-building sessions with respect to facilitation ensures that work goals are accomplished.
3. Check alignment and prepare to get to work.

HPTs are a strong mobilizing influence in each school. In some cases, a small and isolated group of practitioners can plant the seeds in a way that invites their colleagues to the table. Across the CSSR network of schools there is a realization that HPTs are critical to aligning and integrating their work.

CSSR: PROJECT TEAM CHARTER

OVERVIEW

A charter is used to describe the purpose, scope, parameters, and authority structure for the project team. It is essential that every team have a charter! The charter, in addition to creating a clear focus, is a document that is very useful to share with stakeholders for communication and buy-in purposes.

COMPONENTS

A. Purpose: A one or two line statement that describes the key objectives of the team/project.

B. Stakeholder Value Propositions: A clear statement of the value created by the project for key stakeholders (ranked from most important to least with regard to the project purpose).

STAKEHOLDER	VALUE PROPOSITION
• Students	
• Parents	
• Community	
• Teachers	
• Administrators	
•	
•	
•	
•	
•	

C. Interested Parties: A list of individuals and groups, beyond the stakeholders listed above, that have an interest in the project, and who will be kept in the loop re: team progress.

Figure 4.2.   Team charter, page 1. Courtesy of WR Bryan LLC.

D. Communication Requirements: What must be communicated, to whom, how frequently, using what vehicles, etc.

E. Deliverables: A list of outcomes the team will accomplish.

F. Team Members: A list of team members and team roles.

G. Level of Effort: The time commitment required of team members in general, and for members in specific team roles.

H. Governance Structure: The individuals or groups with decision authority regarding the functioning of the team to include the allocation of resources. Provide a project organization chart as necessary. Internal decision making process can also be described here.

I. Authority: What the team has the final word on.

J. Interdependencies: Individuals and/or other teams/groups that this team must interact with to be successful.

K. Data Sources: A list of internal and external data sources relevant to the mission of the team.

L. Action Steps: A list of major steps and scheduled milestones that delineate the process and timeline the team will follow to meet its objectives.

M. Measures of Success: Well-defined measures employed to assess the success of the team, as well as to measure progress along the way.

N. Contact Schedule: Meeting/contact schedule(s), type of work performed, and with whom.

Figure 4.3.   Team charter, page 2.

Implementing for Fidelity and Sustainability

When you unleash the potential of leaders to create the conditions for organizational growth and development, a school becomes a dynamic learning environment for everyone involved and there is broad ownership across the building and beyond. As Peggy Reynolds, site coordinator at Nashua High School North and Nashua High School South, said, *"There is no way for this work not to continue. Teachers are invested in it now!"*

Networking as a Shared Leadership Strategy

As discussed in more detail in chapter 3, shared leadership opportunities across a network or district allow schools to move out of isolation into a wider community of learners. Gregg Sinner, Ph.D., CSSR school change coach, saw the main triumph of the project being a demonstration that *"schools can derive support from each other across schools and across districts."*

Cross-district work came in the form of three intentional learning communities: The Performance Assessment Working Group, Performance Assessment Review Board, and Summer Institute. Through these ongoing communities of practice, shared leadership emerged as team members refined their skills and owned the change process together. Cross-site work carried over to the school-based teams as members of the i3 New England Network were more comfortable leading change in their own schools.

FINAL REFLECTIONS

The two key lessons about leadership in general and shared leadership in particular are, first, that culture change takes time and doesn't happen in a linear fashion and, second, that if leadership is shared across the organization change might happen beneath the surface but not become visible for some time. The time necessary to embed new leadership practices in schools usually takes up to five years. It is important to know that much of the progress is only fully manifested in years 4 and 5 of the change.

Shared leadership helps create the conditions that enable people's authentic voices to be heard and unleashes not only individual genius, but also the collective genius of the school community at large.

NOTE

1. A. Deutschman, May 2005, "Change or Die," Fast Company, retrieved at www.fastcompany.com/52717/change-or-die.

Chapter Five

Student Agency

"The student body will surprise you. They are smarter than you think and all you have to do is give them the keys. They might crash at first, but eventually they will learn to drive and they will impress you with where they end up."— Ryan Marquis, Pittsfield (New Hampshire) Middle School graduate, class of 2015

Schools must create a set of conditions in which students are empowered to become key partners in the decision-making process about issues that affect their daily experiences in school.

In fall 2010, members of a group of highly regarded and respected educators and advocates for student-centered learning in the country—the New England Network for Personalization and Performance (NENPP)—sat around a conference table to plan a student-centered summer institute. The network had just been awarded a prestigious five-year Investing in Innovation Grant (i3) by the federal government, and the air was electric with anticipation. You could feel the energy and passion of the caring and high aspirations of the group to make authentic change for the 11,000 plus students in the NENPP—change that would transform the learning environments by creating school cultures that personalized learning and led to deepening the student experience through demonstrations of mastery through authentic performance assessment.

The opportunity to bring teachers, students, and school administrators together for three days of rigorous training and courageous conversations before the start of the school year would provide a strong foundation for coaching and professional development. Also, by creating the conditions to allow all voices to be heard and be engaged in the change process, we would increase buy-in and decrease the high levels of resistance that surface early on in the change process. Where we were all motivated by the same desire to make change and better the lives of students, surprisingly, it became apparent that most of the group was not ready to accept that change required that students be at the table from the very beginning of the change process. The pushback to student involvement was strong!

At the core of the NENPP was a strong belief that achievement and engagement will increase when students are provided authentic learning experiences that connect to their own interests and passions and do so at their own pace. Learning anytime, anyplace, and at any pace was the rallying cry used to emphasize the need to rethink learning and teaching. In order to be successful, ownership of learning needed to be placed in the hands of students; teachers became the facilitators of knowledge while students created their own pathways. If everyone was in agreement with this approach, why was there so much pushback?

In education, there are two things that people dislike: change, and the way things currently are. This "great contradiction" has become a major obstacle to implementing authentic student agency in our schools. On one hand, stakeholders emphasize the need for students to be more ambitious and engaged in the learning. On the other, the traditional mindset that the role of the teacher is as a deliverer of information and not a facilitator of knowledge leads some to fear that they may soon become insignificant in the classroom. This fear often prevents many from handing over control of the learning to their students.

For the NENPP team, the consensus was that students should be active members in the redesign process, just not yet. If not now, when? How can we transform a learning environment without involving students in the process? It was this mentality, the traditional mind-set that says we will do what is best for kids, but allow all decisions to be made by the adults, that has been the biggest obstacle and contradiction in public education today.

All change will meet with resistance. If you are not facing resistance, you are not changing anything. So, it is understandable that a team of educators would be reluctant to include students in planning and conducting major changes in their schools. Overcoming the well-meaning resistance in traditional schools toward personalization and performance, it is imperative to lead with students.

In the end, after all the counterarguments were made, all at the table saw the transformative value in engaging students in meaningful ways up front. The most caring and dedicated educators believe that they know their students well enough to plan new initiatives for their students. But, when students are asked to be in the planning conversations, the adults realize that there are things that their students bring to the conversation that expand on the adults' understanding of student interests and desires.

The necessity of involving students became very clear to a concerned group of educators at Har-Ber High School in Springdale, Arkansas. When students were added to the team planning to implement an advisory program, the goals for the program shifted. During this planning process, the adults came to realize that they knew their students well, but not well enough. They learned that including the students in the conversation added much to the understanding that is necessary to adequately and completely address student needs and aspirations. The result of including the student voice was a much better plan.

The opportunity to make authentic change required disrupting the status quo and having the hard conversations with teachers, administrators, and students all in the same room. Providing students with a voice in and out of the classroom that they never knew they had empowered each of them with the skills to channel that voice and influence what they learn, when they learn, and how they learn it. Personalizing the school culture that leads to deeper performance assessments would be the result of true student agency.

As the work progressed, it became clear that involving students early on in any project creates the traction needed for change. Their voice blossomed into opportunities that allowed each of them to choose how they wanted to learn, and when. By increasing voice and choice, students collaborated with teachers to create joint opportunities for governance—having real control over decision making, hiring, and program development.

WHAT IS STUDENT AGENCY?

How do learning environments embrace student agency in a way that allows students to create their own pathways and be engaged, allowing the deepest learning and involvement possible? Student agency is more than having a voice; it is about creating the conditions to allow students the opportunity to have control over what happens in their school and their learning.

The irony of school life is that the students at the center of the educational enterprise are the least empowered members of the community. Without opportunities for students to create their own voice and influence what learning could look like in their communities, students will have an educational experience that lacks substance, purpose, and relevance. In order to better serve students, schools must create a set of conditions in which students are empowered to become key partners in the decision-making process about issues that affect their daily experiences in school.

In the ideal student-centered environment, student input is sought, listened to, and addressed authentically. Programs, organizations, and structures in the school share the vision that all students deserve the opportunity to have voice and choice, and recognize that young people are capable of participating, leading, and taking action in the school community. Students can become the chief architects of their learning, and contributing citizens to the school community. Schools that embrace student agency drastically improve learning environments where teachers are facilitators of knowledge and all students are prepared for life after high school.

Student agency is based on the idea that every student can uniquely contribute to the successful transformation of the learning community if given the right opportunities. The following conditions promote the development of student agency in the classroom.

Opportunities to develop and express a personal voice. Students must have the chance to express their ideas as they gradually form and engage in dialogue that can connect different perspectives and facilitate new solutions to challenges in the learning environment.

Chance to belong to a working group. Students are empowered when working with other individuals—teachers and students—to effect positive change in the learning environment.

Adult advocates. A productive relationship with a trusted adult is critical for students to feel known and valued in their school.

Learning choice. Students increase their sense of personal competence through a variety of experiences both in and out of the classroom. Students have the opportunity to decide what they learn, *and* how they learn it. Connecting these varied learning experiences helps students build value and direction for their personal paths.

By promoting student agency up-front and early on in the change process, schools begin to see that the engagement and empowerment create a sense of confidence and ownership. Students become advocates for improving their school experience while simultaneously gaining greater levels of academic achievement. The engagement can begin by asking student participants one simple question up-front: When you graduate high school, what do you want to know?

Students have overwhelmingly cited the development of critical skills necessary to be well-rounded members of the twenty-first-century global society. In doing so, the students set the expectations for not only their involvement, but for the involvement and level of effort initiated by all stakeholders. Students set the bar for accountability for the entire change project, and make their desire for increased agency well known. Once students become involved, the change process tends to gain traction and accelerate. Schools discover that student and adult partnerships, in particular, will always shift the climate and culture of a school.

The value of including student voice as a catalyst for innovative change is evident in Minnetonka (Minnesota) High School. Each school year starts with "The Big Hunt for Ideas," where students and staff are invited to suggest project ideas to innovate the learning environment. The annual cycle of innovation carries on to select several projects to focus on for the year, all led by students, which are tested and evaluated to determine impact and scalability. Furthermore, each of the innovative projects follows a lean startup model with no financial investment in project ideas until they are proven worthy.

Student agency begins with adult/student relationship building, which must be cultivated over time and never rushed, especially at the start of a project. It is important to remember that when building adult/student relationships within the context of increasing student agency, the role of the student and teacher in this situation is very different compared to the traditional working relationship. Students are used to being passive voices in the school environment and teachers are the ones who deliver instruction.

When working in a more collaborative environment, students and teachers are in a partnership that builds a sense of trust and respect through a series of team development activities and sharing opportunities. In this environment, students and teachers must feel safe to take risks, share concerns, and challenge each other to better the school culture for everyone.

Many students and teachers are products of their own system, a system that is obsolete and traditional—a system where student voice is seldom thought to be included in discussion that goes beyond student social issues. On the surface, these may be viewed as important activities to the overall school culture, but they do not get to the depth of student agency. True student agency allows students and teachers to explore what is possible for the school as a whole.

By understanding various strategies, and how each one has been customized to meet the unique needs of the learning environment, students and teachers can develop an approach that is school specific and maximizes the strengths and assets already in place. Site visits, student forums, and assessments are different vehicles to be explored. Just like any school change initiative, this takes time but, if done well, will produce culture-changing results.

Schools may embrace the philosophy of student agency but differ in their implementation based on unique school, community, and student needs. Changes will be gradual, and individual sites will progress at their own pace. You can't rush relationship building! The road traveled will have essential rest stops: the process starts with understanding their current capacity for student agency, then explores what is possible through school visits and student shadowing, and ends with student agency taking on a different look and definition in each learning environment—but the tools in each of our travel bags will look very different.

In order to advance the development of student agency in any learning environment, the following four practices should be considered: (1) governance; (2) leadership and advocacy; (3) purposeful advisory programs; and (4) creating a culture of student agency. These practices are overlapping and interrelated; it is useful to consider them separately—understanding that each contributes to a whole that is greater than the sum of its parts.

SCHOOL GOVERNANCE

Part of the vision for a student-driven school is one where the governing body—made up of students democratically elected by a majority of their peers—is empowered with making school-based policy. Students, acting as the governing body of the school, are making decisions that go well beyond issues impacting bake sales or hallway procedures. Rather, students are provided the opportunity and responsibility to influence all aspects of the learning environment, including decision making and authority around practice, procedures, and operating structures. Students involved in these governing bodies make decisions that have a direct impact on the entire school community.

The site council at Pittsfield (New Hampshire) Middle High School is an exemplar of student governance and agency. At the request of students, community members, and administrators, Pittsfield's school board agreed to create a site council that includes ten students and nine adults. Through a series of planning workshops, the council crafted a team charter, researched exemplars, created and adopted bylaws, and garnered community support. The Pittsfield Community Site Council held its first official meeting in early May 2011. Since that time, they have effected the following school-wide changes: determined the structures of their advisory program, approved a flexible schedule providing more opportunities for student and teacher creativity, and created a restorative justice program.

> "My work with the Site Council opened up an unimaginable amount of opportunities. The skills I gained through my work are those that aren't taught in the classroom. They're built through experience and trust. I'm sure it takes a lot on the faculty's part to trust a group of students to make decisions regarding their education. As I said in my speech at graduation 'The student body will surprise you. They're smarter than you think. All you have to do is give them the keys. They might crash first, but eventually they'll learn how to drive, and they'll impress you with where they end up.'"—Ryan Marquis, recent Pittsfield High graduate

Transformational student-led governing bodies differ greatly from traditional student governance structures that typically conduct work focused on social events rather than educational matters, and don't typically include a representative body of students. Structures like the Pittsfield Site Council become embedded into the fabric of the school culture and community, where adults value and act on the voices of students.

Will, a recent graduate of Plymouth North High School (PNHS) in Plymouth, Massachusetts, describes the energy student voice and agency provides as "a disease"; once it starts, it takes over the entire school building. PNHS, which had an existing student council at the start of 2011, held numerous student engagement community forums and gradually amplified student voice within the existing structures. They have dramatically re-worked their student council to better align with the belief that schools must create conditions where all students' input is sought, listened to, and acted upon. Among their innovations was the creative use of technology and social media to receive input from the student body and communicate their work. Making the commitment to be more inclusive of student viewpoints in shaping transformative practices and policies is a risk, but one that has been proven to drastically change a learning environment in a way that will result in increasing academic achievement for most students. The risk stirs up fears and emotions that are involved in any change impacting human behavior and educational philosophy: for the adults in the building, handing over control to teenagers is both an unknown and a loss. Not knowing how students will react to a sense of autonomy and newly granted leadership at first is like sending a ship out to sea without a working engine—the forces of nature control the actions; ambiguity must be accepted. For adults, they do not fear change, but instead, loss.

Providing students with a say in governance decisions leads some to question their own abilities and role within the school culture; many teachers wonder if their position will eventually become obsolete. Teachers are the facilitators of knowledge in the classroom and will always be the gatekeepers to providing students with the opportunities to be empowered, engaged, and excited about learning. That said, in a student-driven environment promoting authentic agency, the role of the teacher may change, but their influence becomes greater than ever before.

Schools can't hand over the keys without extensive training, structured conversations, and systemic changes to habits, routines, practices, and pro-cess. Pittsfield Middle High School was intentional about providing their students with legitimate governance opportunities. The result is students with more ownership of their schools, and a greater awareness of the many factors involved in shared decision making. At the end of the day, the students have been given authentic experiences in citizenship and the democratic process. They have developed valuable skills and competencies in communication and collaboration. It is noteworthy that these changes require very little in the way of fiscal resources and have paid huge dividends in student and school outcomes.

LEADERSHIP AND ADVOCACY

Leadership and advocacy are close cousins of school governance. They represent a shift in mind-set—asking students to become active and committed citizens in their school and to not only speak about issues, but to influence stakeholders on issues such as education policy and redesign. The impact of embracing student leadership and advocacy extends beyond the walls of the learning environment, and impacts decision making throughout the community and in other neighboring districts. This shift in mind-set values students as *resources* for the school, rather than *products* of the school.

Sometimes a simple comment can be enough to compel a school to reexamine its priorities; sometimes, a simple comment is so powerful that it impacts the hearts and minds of teachers and administrators and forever transforms a school and district.

Abbey McIntosh, a student at Nashua High School South in Nashua, New Hampshire, is a perfect example of how students can influence change. After participating in a youth voice activity where she and fellow students from Nashua High School South concluded that the level of student participation at the school was tokenism, Abbey, as the spokesperson for the group, stood up in front of three dozen educators and told the group: "We rank at the level of tokenism!" Nashua principal Keith Richards remembers the moment saying, "It was a shot to my heart." Project leader Peggy Reynolds said, "We heard the word, and knew she was right. The student involvement was not meaningful." Abbey's opinion was not only heard, but was quickly acted upon at both district high schools.

The moment was transformative for the Nashua School District; district and school leaders began to radically rethink student voice. One of their first steps was to include students in planning sessions about creating a more personalized school environment for students. The result was E-Block, a thirty-five-minute period of time set aside each day for academic support. It allows for students to complete work, see teachers for extra help, and engage in enrichment opportunities. This was the school's attempt to provide equitable opportunities for all students, many of whom could not readily access afterschool academic support programs, or clubs and activities, because of family and employment obligations. The involvement of students in the creation, planning, and proposal phase played a key role in getting this major schedule adjustment approved by the Board of Education.

Student support and enthusiasm for new programs can often sway adult opinions and get broad-based support. Nashua students continue to be involved in conversations about policy change. The district has invited students to weigh in on changes impacting grading and reporting policies, class rank, and twenty-first-century skill building. A student-led team recently translated the twenty-first-century skills into student-friendly language that was adopted into policy. Student leadership and advocacy went beyond enriching the conversations to guiding them, including the creation of rubrics to assess whether students were mastering those skills.

Abbey recognizes that her comment "profoundly touched them." The moment changed her entire high school experience and allowed her to better understand the leadership structure at both the school and district level, and how students can have an authentic voice in those structures. Over the past three years, teachers and administrators continually brought up Abbey's comment as part of a commitment to making sure that the transformational change in Nashua was purposeful and focused on increasing the level of student engagement at all times.

CREATING A PURPOSEFUL ADVISORY PROGRAM

A strong advisory program where every student is connected with an adult in small groups can be one of the most effective vehicles for developing student agency. Advisories are an important part of ensuring that all students are well served and a leading indicator for improved learning outcomes. Advisories serve many purposes—from simply being a place where students can talk to a trusted adult to a place where personal learning plans and portfolios of student work are developed and assessed.

Powerful advisory programs energize and engage students in their own learning in a more personalized way. Schools can and should use advisory programs as part of a planned and concerted effort to engage the entire school community in meaningful and actionable conversations about transforming the school's culture and climate into a more personalized, performance-driven learning environment.

Putting students at the center of the planning process makes them the chief architects of their learning experience. Advisory programs to support student agency are most effective when they include the development of personal learning plans (PLPs) and student-led conferences (SLCs). PLPs support each student's journey through high school by providing a systemic way of guiding students to examine who they are by exploring their talents, interests, and aspirations—and linking these to their learning experiences (coursework, extended learning opportunities, career exploration, etc.). SLCs are a platform for students to publicly take ownership of their learning plans and outcomes, and share them with an advisor, parent/guardian, and sometimes even a member of the larger community (see figure 5.1).

Many schools use advisory programs to support PLPs and SLCs. These schools realized dramatically greater parent participation for SLCs than previously seen for traditional parent-teacher conferences. By hosting the conference and referencing the PLP document, students do most of the talking and learn to articulate who they are, how they learn, where they are headed, and what they need to do to get there. Giving students the opportunity to advocate for themselves in this way is an important part of helping them take responsibility for their lives after high school (see figure 5.2). In Springdale,

Student Led Conference Task List

Deadline		*Task*	*Check off*
		➤ SLC Prep Part 1-Students are provided with an overview of SLC	☐
		➤ SLC Prep Part 2- Advisees complete invitation/ response card packet	☐ ☐
		➤ SLC Prep Part 3- Review Goal Setting etc.	☐
		➤ *Invitations mailed out*	☐
		➤ SLC Prep Parts 4- Students become familiar with the script	☐
		➤ **ALL WORK FROM EACH SUBJECT AREA FROM 1ST MARKING PERIOD WORK IS IN PORTFOLIO!!!**	☐
		➤ SLC Prep Part 5-Portfolio pieces chosen in advisory class	☐
		➤ SLC Prep Part 6-Students write reflection pieces about their work	☐
		➤ *Deadline for parents to mail back responses*	☐
		➤ Advisors call to confirm appointments with parents and complete scheduling grid	☐
		➤ **All 1st marking period grades must be computed**	☐
		➤ SLC Prep Par 7- Students Pair/Share Practice using Script + Peer Evaluations	☐
		➤ **All grades given to advisors at team meeting**	☐
		➤ Room Setup to accommodate Conference ➤ Evaluation Forms available for Parents ➤ Chairs out in hall for waiting parents	☐ ☐ ☐

Figure 5.1. Student-led conference task list.

Arkansas, the advisory program has been used as the vehicle for implementing SLCs for every student in a district of over 23,000 students.

Schools who took their advisory programs a step further used them to effect transformative change in their learning environments. The development of a student-driven learning environment must begin with relationship building and trust between students and adults. An advisory program creates

STUDENT-LED CONFERENCE SCRIPT

I.   Introduction:

> "Mom…Dad…I would like you to meet my mentor, Mrs. Jones. Mrs. Jones, let me introduce my parents, Betty and Barney Rubble.

II.   Purpose of the SLC: "The purpose of this conference is…"

> … to give me the opportunity to share some of the work samples I have completed in my classes this year and also to show you how I am progressing towards graduation.

III.   Graduation Requirements: "I need to…"

> Fill in graduation requirement here…

IV.   Explain the agenda. "During this conference I will…"

> …show you some work samples and explain what I've been doing in my classes.
> Tell you my grades.
> Explain what I think my strengths and weaknesses are.

V.   Show samples of work you're proud of and/or tell your parents/guardians what you're learning in your classes.

> Student should have a list of all their classes and use grids to note what they will show and discuss.

VI.   Tell parents/guardians what your grades are. Discuss what you see as your major strengths and interest and what your areas of weakness and lack of interest are.

> I usually get A's in English and Language Arts but am having trouble in Algebra…
> I want to know more about how to write and really don't want to do too much more math.

VII.   Conclusion: "Does anyone have any questions?"

> "Would you like to add anything that I have forgotten?"   "Thank you for coming"

Figure 5.2.   Sample student-led conference agenda.

the right conditions and structures for those relationships to develop. However, to fully realize the power of an advisory program, all educators must reflect on their roles in a way that may challenge their core beliefs.

CREATING A CULTURE OF STUDENT AGENCY

Creating student agency requires people in the school community to think and act differently. Identifying the conditions that must be changed in order to fully embrace student agency is a critical first step, and for some schools that means developing collaborative skills for both adults and students. For other schools it means confronting beliefs about teacher and student roles. Each school will have a different set of challenges to contend with as they embark on the work.

Without really stepping back to evaluate conditions, some schools may be able to achieve increased student voice or even engagement, but true student agency requires schools to think more broadly about changing long-standing traditions. Extensive coaching and professional development help create conditions in schools that allow students and adults to have authentic conversations on student agency in a productive way that built on, rather than threatened, long-standing traditions.

FINAL REFLECTIONS

Schools and districts must be ready for numerous challenges when embracing student agency and must share lessons (good and the bad) with colleagues as part of professional learning communities. The biggest challenges involve students and teachers accepting changes to their traditional roles. The traditional structure of schools creates barriers that are hard to overcome.

Successful schools have gone beyond energizing a cohort of students interested in working toward greater student agency. Rather than focusing on groups of students who jump at any opportunity to be more involved, these sites worked diligently to engage all students, especially those who had previously not been successful or trusting in the traditional school environment.

Similarly for educators, moving beyond a group of teachers interested in bolstering student voice and choice to the full faculty can be very challenging. These were typically the teachers who agree to serve on student council or have had success with student voice and choice in their classroom. Before sites were able to build a critical mass of educators ready to embrace student agency, most held a number of difficult conversations before realizing that, rather than giving students the keys to the school, they were giving students the keys to learning and success. As with any major school change initiative, if a site is not dealing with resistance to change, they are really not changing.

Chapter Six

Student-Driven Learning

At its best, student-driven learning enables young people to bring their unique life experiences and interests into the learning environment. Students take ownership for what, how, and even where they learn.

ALLISON'S JOURNEY

The night before the first day of freshman year, Allison lay awake fretting about fitting in, forming new friendships, defining a role on a soccer team, and auditioning for the fall musical. What she didn't consider was just how different her educational experience at Noble High School in North Berwick, Maine, would be.

On the first day of classes, her Earth Science instructor asked a question: "Where do we get our water?" The teacher probed further by asking, "Is all water quality similar? Will we have enough quality water?" Ten minutes later, Allison was collecting water samples from three sources: a local stream, a retention pond on the campus, and the water fountains located inside the school. She worked with three other students to conduct tests on the three samples before analyzing the data and drawing conclusions from their findings. The teacher brought the groups back together using a collaborative discussion protocol where each student was required to share part of their findings. Ten months later, Allison prepared for her end-of-year round-table discussion. Before her parents, her math teacher, and two of her soccer teammates, Allison presented the story of her freshman year and answered three simple questions: (1) Who am I? (2) Where am I going? (3) How will I get there?

Little did Allison know that while the questions would become more rigorous, and the inquiry more sophisticated, the same experiences would manifest during her sophomore year. Her English, math, social studies, and biology teachers began the year by asking all eighty heterogeneously grouped students assigned to Sophomore Team 1: "What is community?" Within the first month of school, she examined the essential question through the lens of each subject area. Her English class incorporated an analysis of community while reading George Orwell's text *Animal Farm*, while her social studies class began analyzing the community envisioned during the writing of the United States Constitution.

At her student-led conference in June, she had a much better idea of who she was and where she was going. She spoke with passion about what strategies she would use during grade 11 and 12 to help prepare her for college.

At the start of junior year, she was working with the Community Engagement Center at Noble to locate authentic learning opportunities related to her potential career interests. She worked with a local technician at a science laboratory and parlayed her job shadows into a summer internship. Real-world experiences gained during the summer served as a springboard for her senior project, which explored the relationship between pesticide use and a waning fish population in Maine's lakes and rivers. Her presentation, delivered to a panel of teachers, students, and experts earned her a designation of Accept with Distinction.

Allison had teachers who understood competencies and authentic, inquiry-based performance assessment. By the close of high school she, like many of her peers, had engaged in four end-of-year student-led conferences, delivered numerous presentations, and engaged in several inquiry-based research projects. Most fundamentally, she was allowed to define what she needed from school. As a result, Allison's high school experience served the dual purpose of building critical twenty-first-century skills and exposing her to enough real-world experiences that she left high school understanding how she could fit into a changing world.

THE STUDENT-DRIVEN APPROACH

Allison's journey would not have been possible in a school that wasn't totally committed to student-driven, deeper learning. The ecosystem described in this book demonstrates how inquiry, student agency, and shared leadership combined can lead to the deeper, student-driven learning that Allison experienced.

Through a focused emphasis on networking within schools and between schools, the learning becomes deeper. Student-driven learning represents the deepest and most engaging kind of learning and is at the heart of personalized learning and teaching. Students bring their unique life experiences and interests into the learning environment. In most schools, where the emphasis is on covering content, those experiences and interests are seldom called upon.

A student-driven learning environment begins with the development of trusting relationships and solid structures that allow all students the opportunity to plan and develop their own personalized pathways. Students take ownership and responsibility for what, how, and sometimes *where* they learn. It offers students the chance to make meaning and connect with the world through rigorous academic experiences—both in and out of school—in a way that builds on their interests as well as their learning needs.

At its best, student-driven learning is authentic, open ended, and problem based; it requires application of skills with clear standards of mastery set in advance. It is thoughtful and reflective—requiring students to synthesize, analyze, and evaluate information toward the creation of new knowledge. This approach is not entirely new, but its efficacy has been fully validated over the past decade by cutting-edge neuroscience.

This large and growing body of research points to the importance of intrinsic motivation in learning. In other words, when students are provided an opportunity to make meaningful choices about what they want to learn, they are more engaged in the learning experience. Greater engagement, in turn, leads to better learning outcomes. In a student-driven learning environment, students develop skills that will prepare them for the demands of a rapidly changing society: the capacity to integrate knowledge, to communicate clearly, to see the relationships and connections among phenomena, and to be responsive to new challenges and ever-changing conditions.

For over two decades, the Center for Secondary School Redesign (CSSR) has focused on creating personalized learning environments in high schools. This vision preceded the advent of both blended learning and competency-based education as options to help secondary schools create the personalized culture that allows the goodness and genius of each and every student to thrive. As one of the early technical assistance providers focused on assisting existing schools to incorporate student-driven learning as the *central* element to school change, CSSR has provided intense support to existing high schools to made dramatic changes in their practices that have resulted in significant progress toward that goal.

Truly effective personalized learning that includes performance assessment is grounded in the *five standards of authentic instruction*: (1) higher-order thinking; (2) depth of knowledge; (3) connectedness to the world beyond the classroom; (4) substantive conversation; and (5) social support for student achievement.[1] Connectedness to the world beyond the classroom provides authenticity and relevance to a student's learning. When completed, the work provides meaning to students beyond complying with the teacher's criteria for evaluation. Student-driven learning depends on the free exchange of substantive dialogue between students and adults, including through student choice in learning and student voice in school governance.

COMPETENCY-BASED EDUCATION

When schools are organized around personalized performance assessments for demonstration of mastery, learning shifts from a standard sequence of courses (adult controlled) to the selection of personally relevant learning activities that lead to unique long-term goals (student controlled). Often these personalized pathways do not fall within the standardized framework that uses seat time as a determinant of course completion (i.e., "credit," or "Carnegie Unit").

Competency-based education (CBE) is growing nationally. In 2005, New Hampshire abolished the Carnegie Unit, mandating that all high schools measure credit according to students' mastery of materials, rather than time spent in class. In 2012, the Maine legislation began requiring public high schools to award diplomas based on demonstrated proficiency—not passing grades and course credit. Now forty-one of the fifty states require or permit requiring mastery for earning high school course credit. In order for CBE to be effective, student progress through demonstrating mastery of competencies along personalized pathways requires validated systems of assessing performance.

A proficiency-based progression differs greatly from the traditional credit-based progression where a grade of D– earns the *same credit* as a grade of A+. Competencies ask what students can *do*, to demonstrate what they *know*. They are aligned to state learning standards such as the Common Core State Standards and Next Generation Science Standards, but also apply to rigorous twenty-first-century workplace, civic, and social skills. Relevance emanates from authentic learning experiences as students, driven by their interests, build knowledge, concepts, and skills connected to their personal goals.

The competency-based approach requires alignment around five key elements: (1) students advance upon demonstrated mastery; (2) competencies include explicit, measurable, and transferable learning objectives; (3) assessment is meaningful and a positive learning experience; (4) students receive rapid, differentiated support based on their individual learning needs; and (5) learning outcomes emphasize competencies that include application and creation of knowledge, along with the development of important skills and dispositions.[2]

PERSONALIZED PERFORMANCE ASSESSMENT

In a student-driven school, the standards are rigorous, and students must demonstrate competency across many subject areas and skill categories. Learning is frequently measured through personalized performance assessments that allow students to master required content while pursuing an area of interest that motivates and engages them in their learning. For example, students can demonstrate their learning by designing and creating an interactive product; proving an idea or concept true or untrue; designing and carrying out experiments; or synthesizing large volumes of information for an authentic audience. Personalized performance assessments differ from more traditional pen and paper assessments or standardized tests in that they connect with student interests in a way that makes learning more purposeful and authentic. Visualize how personalized performance assessments fall on a continuum of assessments.

Performance assessments enable teachers and parents to get a far more detailed and nuanced account of what their students know and are able to do. With that information, they can more easily support their students with targeted learning strategies. Students often report that the work is much harder in a student-driven learning environment, but that it is also far more satisfying because there is greater flexibility in meeting the standards. Performance assessments in a student-driven learning environment provide evidence of student learning, which often compels students to work harder because the work is not an isolated exercise, but something that has enduring value and can be shared with others.

Student-driven-learning provides a vision of the possibilities for student engagement leading to deep learning by exploring the various ways that several schools have implemented personalized performance assessment. However, implementing personalized performance assessments alone did not and most likely would not have resulted in the progress made in those instances. To be sure, these improvements required a much broader effort than simply suggesting that personalized performance assessment could be transformative. Without support to develop inquiry teaching in each classroom, and the development of student agency in school governance, no progress would have been made.

STUDENT-DRIVEN LEARNING OPPORTUNITIES

Classroom culture is a powerful activator of student agency. The classroom is where students spend the majority of their time. Conditions have to be created where personalization and student voice and choice are at the heart of the experience. Student agency is unlikely to flourish in a classroom that is teacher dominated or rigidly structured. This requires a fundamental role shift—teachers facilitate and coach learning, rather than package and deliver learning. Furthermore, administrators must address barriers like bell schedules, graduation requirements, and tracking practices that obstruct efforts to promote change. Finally, students must take responsibility for all aspects of their school experiences and resist the urge to merely be compliant.

Innovative schools have long been encouraged to move away from pencil and paper and embrace authentic learning experiences such as the senior project and/or extended learning opportunity (ELO) as a means for students to direct a large project in pursuit of their interests and passions. These learning opportunities often have a stipulation that they serve the community in some way. Giving students occasions to participate in, and learn from, projects that provide service creates rich conditions for the deepest learning possible, and is a powerful way to engage even the most disenfranchised students. An ELO allows for the primary acquisition of knowledge and skills through instruction or study outside of the traditional classroom methodology, including, but not limited to, apprenticeships, service, internships, online learning, and independent study.

In the following sections, we describe examples of personalized performance assessments. Each school in these examples interpreted this work differently based on their unique school settings. The components of the assessments are similar—requiring students to drive their own learning process by selecting an area of interest and building a learning experience that includes a proposal, a portfolio of work, a product, and a presentation. What made these practices part of the everyday learning environment in each of the schools was a deep and abiding belief system and culture that embraced student-driven learning.

PERSONAL LEARNING PLANS (PLPS) AND STUDENT-LED CONFERENCES (SLCS)

In a student-driven learning environment, each student develops a personal learning plan (PLP) as a formal structure for reflecting on his/her academic and personal development. The PLP contains evidence of learning progress, information about personal strengths and challenges, as well as goals and dreams. Each student is paired with an adviser, who helps guide them on their path to graduation. Given the often-fluctuating interests of adolescents, the PLP does not press the student into prematurely selecting a career path but, rather, makes the space for an ongoing conversation about a student's cognitive, social, and emotional development. The PLP also enables parents and guardians to see inside a student's high school experience and his/her thought processes related to future endeavors.

The PLP also becomes the centerpiece of the student-led conference (SLC) during which time a student shares his/her PLP with a small group that includes an adviser, parent(s), and additional trusted and invested individuals (coaches, pastors, school staff, friends, etc.). The SLC experience holds students accountable to the progress they make toward their short- and long-term goals. Parent attendance at the SLC is dramatically greater than for traditional parent-teacher conferences, a testament to the authentic meaning of the experience. Parents often express joy and surprise at what their children are able to articulate about themselves, and students assume much greater ownership for their learning when they are genuinely held accountable to their community.

The superintendent of schools in Springdale, Arkansas, was asked to identify the one thing his district should consider doing to make real change. The response was to implement student-led conferences. Springdale, the second-largest school district in Arkansas with over 22,000 students, has successfully been implementing for the past several years student-led conferences for all its students. In kindergarten through grade 2, the conferences are student involved rather than student led; grades 3 through 12 are implementing true student-led conferences.

The learning form Springdale concludes that SLCs are proving to be an effective method to connect each student to their educational experience based on personal interests, strengths, and goals to improve. Significantly, the district is finding it to be a purposeful and meaningful use of time and resources when used in the context of other personalized learning strategies.

District leadership additionally concluded that when students are involved parents/guardians come to school, and students express pride in their ability to share their accomplishments and goals. Survey data from parents concerning their son or daughter's SLCs are very positive, with about 80 percent of parents agreeing that they learned something about their child that they didn't know before the SLC. The Springdale schools also see the SLC as a great public relations tool—parents are learning a lot about what goes on academically at school from their child.

Comments gathered from the Springdale surveys include such statements as "This is the first time I have spent this much time with my child talking about what goes on at school," "I have learned things about my child that I never knew before," and "I have learned a lot about what my child is learning at school."

EXTENDED LEARNING OPPORTUNITIES (ELOS)

Many schools offer extended learning opportunities as one way of demonstrating mastery of required competencies (or earning course credit). Extended learning opportunities (ELOs) are a form of self-directed learning in which students access learning experiences in a field of their choice outside of the traditional classroom. Students are supported by a school-based adviser, and in many cases, students also have a mentor who is based in the community and embedded in their field of interest. These "anywhere, anytime" learning experiences are uniquely rigorous, and can include apprenticeships, community service, independent study, online coursework, internships, job shadowing, performance, or private instruction.

Beginning in 2007, the New Hampshire Department of Education, with funding from the Nellie Mae Education Foundation, began developing four comprehensive ELO pilot sites. Since then, the state has been a leader in the development and articulation of ELO programming. The state recognizes four components of an ELO that result in the highest levels of academic and personal learning for students: (1) research; (2) reflection; (3) product; and (4) presentation. These four components allow multiple opportunities for both formative assessment (as the ELO is occurring) and summative assessment (in the culminating product and presentation). Most ELO programs have common rubrics for assessing the uncommon activities associated with the individual experiences, as shown by the following:

Key Assessment Criteria for ELOs and Senior Projects

Students will demonstrate their learning through research, reflection, product, and presentation.

Research

During the learning process, the student will build his/her base of knowledge through research as he/she develops proficiency in his/her targeted competencies. Research consists of an active search for new information and knowledge, which includes a focused idea or essential question (EQ); an organized set of personal experiences, which can expand or constrain his/her initial understanding; and the analysis, synthesis, and communication of these experiences.

Reflection

Reflections allow students the opportunity to think about, make meaning of, and analyze their experiences to "get the learning out" of these experiences. Through reflection, students develop and adjust their short- and long-term goals, explore problems and solutions encountered during their learning, and *connect* their experiences to their learning goals.

Reflections are an important part of the feedback loop between the student and the certified school personnel and, if applicable, mentor. Therefore, sharing the learning with the certified school personnel and mentor in a timely manner allows the student to receive formative guidance through timely responses to the reflection, increasing his/her learning.

Product

The application of the student's learning consists of the process of designing, creating, implementing, and assessing a product, which will be an artifact or event that the student uses to demonstrate the culmination of his/her learning and/or achievement of competencies related to the learning experience. Targeted goals, competencies, and an essential question are identified at the beginning of the student's learning experience. The product will be an original piece of work designed to promote the student's personal growth and/or to benefit a larger community.

The product can be a physical artifact in any appropriate medium. It can be a live or recorded event or a demonstration of skill/competency. The product may be a process, developing an original design of a device, procedure, or system. The product should meet standards of quality work deemed appropriate to the student's level of experience by the certified school personnel and/or mentor. The product will be shared with an authentic audience within an authentic context.

Presentation

The presentation is designed to assess the student's ability to clearly communicate his/her growth during the learning experience to an audience that could include members who are either expert or novice in the disciplines related to the student's learning goals and/or essential question.

The presentation should describe the nature of the student's learning experience: his/her goals, essential question, and his/her growth in the targeted competencies. The student should illustrate the development of this growth during the learning process (documentation). The student should also be able to communicate what he/she learned through the successes and challenges of the learning experience and how he/she changed as a result of it (metacognition).

* * *

Student ownership of the planning and execution of the learning experience are critical components of an ELO. Success is measured by the ability of the students to master competencies as they relate to the chosen field of study as evidenced through the presentation at the end of the experience. This process requires students to make a connection between the competencies and the activities that led to mastery. Metacognition through reflection is a complex process that deepens students' understanding of the work and themselves.

ELOs are offered for as many reasons as there are interested students. Each student brings to the experience his/her own story, and ELOs add to those stories by shaping students' learning pathways and future goals. ELOs have thrived and are now a key element of schools and districts across North America. Wm. E. Hay Composite High School in Stettler, Alberta, provides ELOs for all its students. Students in the i3 New England Network successfully completed numerous ELOs, including the following sampling: job shadowing at a physical therapy office; restoration of an antique tractor; learning sign language; interning at a local newspaper; serving as an assistant DJ for a local radio station; working with the police department's forensic division; learning tae kwon do; and learning a musical instrument.

Because of this variability of ELOs, several common structures were critical to their success. First, each school designated an "owner" of the ELO program who provided oversight for the ongoing ELO projects—coordinating the diverse ELO placements in the community; ensuring that students were accounted for and safe while working outside of the school building; planning for professional development and compensation for teachers serving as ELO advisers; and so forth. Second, each school put in place a well-vetted process for planning and assessing ELOs (see the planning document example in figures 6.1, 6.2, and 6.3) and validating scores including through the calibration of rubrics and reviewing artifacts of student work in professional learning communities.

Third, schools shifted their schedules to accommodate students' placements in ELO sites without compromising their other coursework. Finally, an intentional system of support was created so that students practiced important life skills that would serve them beyond high school. These four structures enabled adults and students to stretch and grow through an ongoing scaffolding process. Below are student-driven learning examples:

* * *

Kellie, a senior at Nashua High School South in Nashua, New Hampshire, spent the entire 2014–2015 school year completing an ELO on the Performance Assessment Review (PAR) Board in order to better understand the process of high school redesign and education policy. As part of her project, Kellie participated in multiple school visits, contributed to final reports, and provided the PAR Board with valuable perspective on student-driven learning best practices. Kellie's ELO is a powerful example of a performance assessment that directly resulted in increased student agency in her school.

* * *

Krista, a student at Plymouth North High School in Plymouth, Massachusetts, completed a senior project creating an a cappella group at her district's

Student Name: _____

ELO Title: _____

Step 1: PLANNING (Student and teacher work together)

Standards or Competencies The student and teacher should research the standards or competencies that can be met through the ELO project to establish general expectations and goals for the project. The competencies will have some natural content and skills associated with them. In addition, please list what the student will know and be able to do as a result of this project.	
Project Description The student and teacher should work together to give a detailed description of the project. What is involved? Describe the final product and presentation. Include a broad description of what will be assessed. Include what the product will look like and where and how students will showcase their work.	
The Essential Question The student will develop an essential question which focuses the activity, motivates the student, and drives the learning. It should be broad enough not to be answered easily and can be approached from many different entry points. It lends itself to interdisciplinary research.	**My Essential Question:**
Community partners Identify community partners who offer a rich source of knowledge, refined application, and experience in the project area. Also, describe their role in the project planning, implementation and assessment.	

Figure 6.1.   Extended learning opportunity (ELO) planning tool, page 1.

middle school. Krista demonstrated student agency in three ways: embracing the opportunity to make a choice about the work she was going to do and how she would demonstrate learning; exploring a career area about which

Step 2: Implementation and Formative Assessments

Timeline and Benchmarks **Create a timeline** of benchmark projects that provide a foundation for the final project. Benchmark projects can be small, discreet projects, rehearsals, practices, drafts or other work that allows the student to move towards competency. Students should have ample opportunities to have work reviewed before the final presentation, a timeline should be established.	
Reflection Identify structures that guarantee student input and reflection is captured along the way. Ask students to reflect on their progress in the class, and have them self-assess benchmark projects with relation to the larger, final project. **List what methods** students will use for reflection and self-evaluation.	
Teacher/student communication Teacher and student should establish together **how and how often** the student will communicate with the HQT.	
Community partner communication Describe how regular communications with the community partner will take place. Community partners should be part of the student reflection so they can see students' developing understanding. Describe how the community partner will participate in the assessment of the project.	

Figure 6.2.   Extended learning opportunity (ELO) planning tool, page 2.

she was curious; and creating an experience that served more than twenty students in her community.

* * *

Hanzla, a student from Nashua High School North in Nashua, New Hampshire, created and helped implement a mentoring program where older

Step 3: Summative Assessment

Final Project	
Describe in detail what the final project will include, what will be assessed, and who will assess each component. Identify common assessment goals that will be met during the final project. As the project develops, these goals may be modified through negotiation between the Highly Qualified Teacher and the student. Assessors will be given the assessment rubric at least one week in advance with a brief description of the final project and will be informed as to what competencies they are assessing.	

ELO Presentation	
Preliminarily identify when the final presentation on your ELO will occur. You should also have a sense of who will be on the assessment panel and what, if any, special equipment or facilities you may need access to. All ELO presentations must include the Highly Qualified Teacher, Community Partner (within reason) and ELO coordinator.	

Assessment of the ELO

Following the presentation assessors will be given the opportunity to ask questions. Feedback will be offered to the student. Assessment rubrics and feedback forms will be handed in to the Highly Qualified Teacher at the time of the final presentation and a brief discussion will take place regarding student performance following the presentation.

The Highly Qualified Teacher will review the feedback, meet with the student and submit a grade within one week of the final presentation.

Figure 6.3. Extended learning opportunity (ELO) planning tool, page 3.

students provide support to younger students transitioning into high school. Inspired by Hanzla and his team, the other district high school—Nashua South—joined forces with Nashua North to form Panther and Titan Connection. The program recruits upperclassmen to serve as mentors to incoming ninth graders in both schools. The commitment begins at ninth-grade orientation and extends throughout the year during E-Block. Upperclassmen were motivated to initiate the program out of their own realization that they had wished for more support when they first entered high school.

* * *

Ryan, a student from Pittsfield Middle High School in Pittsfield, New Hampshire, became involved in his school's site council as a freshman. Through his participation he not only learned key skills for democracy and social advocacy, but also learned about meeting facilitation, development of lesson plans, and tuning of teacher materials. As a senior, Ryan proposed running a Learning Studio course. A Learning Studio is a course offered once per week where students can choose from a diverse selection of mini-seminars, typically facilitated by teachers and community members, that are aligned with required competencies, but allow for a wide range of teacher and student interests to drive the curriculum. Ryan was the first student to lead a Learning Studio, and in the process of doing so he decided to change his future plan from becoming an engineer to becoming a teacher.

* * *

Caleb was a very bright student, but typically was not very engaged in the traditional coursework offered at his school. After becoming very interested in an online college lecture series about the brain, Caleb decided to do an ELO on brain functioning. The ELO was modeled on an independent study in which he viewed the lecture series, summarized the lectures, and met with his adviser to discuss them. His midterm product was a Claymation (a video using clay models) that demonstrated how brain synapses work. His work was very detailed, and he became very adept at using the technology to produce the short film.

Later in the year, Caleb began using his computer skills to develop a multilevel video game. He advocated to earn his required computer credit by learning code and creating software. At the end of the year, he completed a required presentation of his ELO to earn credit in biology and computer science—and used these two ELOs as demonstrations of competency for the introductory art class. Given the opportunity to demonstrate competency in his own way, he successfully earned credit in three content areas, while engaged in deep learning experiences driven by his own interests.

* * *

Richard ran his own painting business, and with the support of his father he was able to establish a limited partnership. He oversaw all the tasks involved in running a small business: he managed customers and employees; scheduled work; figured out estimates; and wrote up working contracts. He was fully committed to his work, and determined that the painting business would support his college tuition and related expenses. Richard applied the concepts and vocabulary of economics to his work and earned economics course credit through this ELO experience. The credit was valuable, but the experience was invaluable. The ELO presentation turned out to be only the beginning of a lifelong journey that was sparked by a personal interest.

* * *

The projects demonstrated above are powerful examples of rich learning experiences driven by students. There are several ideal conditions for sites to consider when using student agency to drive learning. Sites must promote a culture of collaboration with and among students and adults, including by intentionally building skills for effective communication. Personal safety for students working outside of the traditional school environment is paramount.

Teachers and students must trust one another, and teachers must make a concerted effort to empower students in all areas. Preparing students for interacting with adults and others outside of the school building requires community access and cultural competence. Above all else, teachers must learn to work as facilitators of learning and embrace anytime, anyplace, any pace learning as a framework for students to drive their own learning experiences.

SENIOR PROJECT

The senior project is a capstone experience for high school seniors to demonstrate a diploma-worthy set of skills and abilities. It is in many ways an ELO required for graduation. Many schools use the senior project as a mechanism to drive students to engage in thoughtful inquiry, and to demonstrate their abilities before an authentic audience. Projects are linked to state standards and frequently tied to competencies. On the eve of their graduation, students are called upon to hone their academic skills, such as reading informational text, writing, research, and public speaking.

Senior projects typically require students to complete a project proposal that defines the topic, states the essential question, and outlines the learning progression—including the final product and exhibition; create a portfolio including a research paper, as well as document correspondence with project mentors, reflections, and signed agreements; develop a product that demonstrates mastery of the topic—these vary widely depending on the scope of the project, for example, a musical piece; hosting a fundraiser; or a prototype; and present a final exhibition in which students answer the essential question, reflect on their experiences—both good and not so good—and deliver a lecture in front of a juried panel.

These projects enable students—as well as teachers, peers, and others—to take ownership of a substantial piece of work, thereby signaling an important coming-of-age milestone.

High school seniors tend to be the most vociferous advocates of the senior project, often commenting that the experience prepared them well for post-secondary life, as expressed by these two students:

> "I found myself learning a lot more than just my topic though. It helped me learn how I work the best, allowed me to become more confident in public speaking and how to properly research, all of which I have found extremely helpful in college."—Noble High School graduate Rebecca Cosgrove

> "The senior project allows a student to explore at least one of the possibilities they see in their future, and they're granted access to valuable resources like teachers who can provide research help, experts in the field, and real-world experiences. High school needs more of these kinds of projects, if anything."—Noble High School graduate Matt Wood

FINAL REFLECTIONS

- Student-driven learning presents a vision for what is possible for student engagement and deeper learning.
- The learning and teaching is structured around the concept that students bring into the learning environment their unique experiences (tangible and intangible) and strengths to build on and contribute to their own learning.
- Each student has the opportunity to learn through flexible times and opportunities; the development of extended learning opportunities (ELO) begins with student passions and desires.
- Performance assessments are at the core of putting students at the center of their own learning. At the heart of this work are projects that are student generated.
- The learning in and out of the classroom is collaborative in nature and includes regularly structured opportunities for reflection, feedback, and refinement.
- Moderation of student scores is the vehicle to ensure that the deepest learning possible is occurring—a vehicle for demonstration of knowledge.
- The learning is deeper, as students demonstrate mastery through a competency-based approach. Personalized exhibitions, portfolios, and other gateways require students to initiate, design, conduct, analyze, revise, and present their work in multiple ways; there is common scoring for uncommon learning tasks.

NOTES

1. Fred Newmann and Gary Wehlage, "Five Standards of Authentic Instruction," *Educational Leadership* 50, no. 7 (April 1993): 8–12.

2. Chris Sturgis, Susan Patrick, and Linda Pittenger, *It's Not a Matter of Time: Highlights from the 2011 Competency-Based Learning Summit*, July 2011, http://www.inacol.org/resource/its-not-a-matter-of-time-highlights-from-the-2011-competency-based-summit/.

Chapter Seven

Creating an Ecosystem for Student-Driven Learning

This chapter addresses laying out the challenge to readers to go into their communities and do what they can to improve the learning experience for their youth.

There is a vast array of potential entry points for creating a more student-driven school and classroom environment, but many seeds must be planted before lasting change can take root. For some schools, personal learning plans and student-led conferences can be a first step toward putting students in the driver's seat of their own learning. Other schools might explore the articulation of competencies and inquiry-based teaching. Still others may be ready to move toward demonstration of mastery through personalized performance assessment.

The ecosystem of school change presented in figure 7.1 represents a way of guiding change for a school to become both student centered and a school where deeper learning is the norm.

A *culture of inquiry* encourages students and teachers to exercise and amplify their authentic voices, and to return to what comes so naturally to very young children: asking their own questions.

Student agency ensures that students have the opportunity to govern their school beyond token contributions, and to exercise their voice as part of the day-to-day running of the school. This looks different in each school because context is all important, but the value of full student participation is consistent across every location.

The *power of a network* allows schools to share challenges and support each other with peer mentoring and to receive outside professional support that validates their strengths, helps manage their challenges, and helps them grow as professionals.

The Ecosystem of Student Driven Learning:

Culture of Inquiry	Power of Network	Shared Leadership	Student Agency	Student Driven Learning
A set of conditions that exist within a school or district in which the focus of learning for students and adults is around answering important and compelling questions	Intentional design choices to harness the power of networking—employing skilled facilitative leadership to support each site.	Creating leadership "density"—beyond those in "positional" authority—can greatly accelerate the change process.	A set of conditions in which students are empowered to become key partners in the decision-making process about issues that affect their daily experiences in school.	At its best, student driven learning enables young people to bring their unique life experiences and interests into the learning environment. Students take ownership for what, how, and even where they learn.

Figure 7.1.   The ecosystem of student-driven learning.

Shared leadership is necessary because of the frequent turnover of those in positions of authority and because those who exercise leadership—whether students, teachers, principals, superintendents, or others—are co-owners of the change process. This assures the long-term sustainability of the change efforts.

Student-driven learning provides the opportunity for students to become partners in their school experience, leading to deeper learning through strong student engagement.

Where to begin to address the five elements for creating student-centered learning depends on where you fit within the school culture. Each of these elements as laid out in chapters 2 through 6 can be implemented on its own as an appropriate starting point to bringing about real student-centered cultures. The greatest impact is achieved if all of the gears are running together, but anyone can both bring about real change for students and start a process that will result in the deepest, most personalized learning for each and every student in a school or district.

STUDENTS

Students can begin by exercising their voice with school administrators and teachers to find ways to enhance their school experience. To lead to meaningful change, the students should exercise their agency in ways that can lead to improving the school climate. Rather than complaining about the food in the cafeteria, they should focus on ways that will improve their learning experience in a deeper, more meaningful way. For example, they can remind building leaders that one of the best ways for students to take ownership of their learning is for them to be included in parent-teacher conferences. They could also make this request directly to their parents.

At the core, students should see that they have a role to question the status quo in all aspects of their school experience; they should ask teachers and administrators, "Why are we doing this?" Explanations that are steeped in tradition are unacceptable. Just because things have always been done a certain way is no reason to assume that there isn't a better way to do things. Asking students to trust in a process or practice without showing the relevance to each student is a sure way to create a disengaged group of students.

TEACHERS

As demonstrated in chapter 2, moving to a culture of inquiry and an inquiry-based approach to classroom pedagogy fosters the opportunity for students to develop their voice through engaged dialogue in the classroom. This will also provide students with the experience needed to be able to make good choices. Reflecting on the choices they've made in the classroom can also provide students with the ability to learn from their mistakes through deep reflection. Teachers embarking on an inquiry-based approach in their classroom will encourage students to exercise their voice and choice in meaningful ways that can lead to increased student agency.

Teachers can also begin a dialogue that is supportive of improving practice by asking other teachers to support them through collegial conversations
that allow teacher professionalism to flourish. Individual teachers will then
be able to not only improve their own practice but will be creating a culture
of inquiry that encourages reflective feedback by all involved. These collaborative conversations are best implemented when students are included in the
groups. Students provide a different perspective that is often missed by otherwise well-meaning and informed teachers.

SCHOOL ADMINISTRATORS

School leaders should begin by accurately assessing the existing culture of
the school and the capacity for change. The existing culture can be assessed
best by two means. One is to engage in student shadowing as described in
chapter 2. The other is to ask those involved to decide on a course of action
by taking an inventory of where each individual feels the school's current
reality is. The continua presented back in chapter 1, in figure 1.1, is a reliable
guide for those conversations. Engaging in these activities will assist building leaders to plot a course that is based on the perceptions of the existing
school culture as the base to build on.

The complexity of the leadership challenge in moving from one practice
to the next is also demonstrated in figure 1.1 by the numbers inserted in the
continua between practices, with level 3 representing the most challenging
and level 1 the least. For many stakeholders, the level-3 transitions reflect the
fact that the change identified may be contrary to their core beliefs about
schooling.

For example, it is often difficult for teachers to accept that their role needs
to change and that they should no longer be the imparter of knowledge, but
the facilitator of learning. Similarly, students won't automatically embrace
agency. Many adolescents would prefer to be anonymous and unknown to
the adults in their school building. Teachers and students need to make
changes that aren't necessarily what teachers signed up for when they became teachers or what students expect from the schooling experience.

So, leaders need to be aware of these challenges and be mindful that the
changes proposed can be seen as a broken promise. However, once the transformational inventory has been completed, plotting a course for change can
include a few relatively easy to implement first steps. These first steps can be
used to assist each individual to understand how their role will transform as
the school transforms. Most will accept their new role after some initial
reticence.

It's important to note that none of the suggested practices we presented
here require any change in state or federal policy. Everything suggested in

this volume has been implemented in schools across the country and has taken place within existing state and federal guidelines. So, building leaders should feel free to support the implementation of the practices presented here.

Redesigning the bell schedule is often a good first step in bringing about the culture shift to put students at the center of their learning. We know that the schedule can incorporate what the school community prioritizes. In crafting the schedule, the first priority should be to include time for teachers to engage in relationship-building conversations with students in an adviser-advisee period. Common planning time should also be prioritized so that all teachers will be able to engage in regular, collegial conversations with their peers.

Building administrators could also consider creating a student advisory committee to inform the building leader about issues that are important to students. Staying closely connected with all students is a central facet of creating true student-centered environments that support student agency and deeper learning. Over time, the advisory committee could be given real authority and, in essence, become the legislative body for the school. We have seen this level of student engagement in several high schools and have witnessed the significant improvement in student agency that results.

DISTRICT ADMINISTRATORS

The best method of bringing about the kind of changes we've discussed here is for district leaders to provide school leaders with the autonomy to implement changes in a manner that they feel will work best in their individual school. That does not mean that the school is free to do whatever the building leader wants. For example, the superintendent could provide a mandate that every student be involved in a student-led conference each semester. But then, each school should have flexibility in how to go about implementing this effort.

The district should offer the opportunity to provide the networking experiences offered through performance assessment work groups, as described in chapter 3. This sharing of ideas and practices can serve to expand the vision of possibilities for all students, teachers, and administrators across district lines or within districts.

COMMUNITY MEMBERS

Community members should become more engaged in the learning process. The wisdom that community members can provide is often missing for students, especially for students who are the first in their family to have aspirations for a postsecondary learning experience. Volunteering to mentor students who are engaged in extended learning opportunities (ELOs) or senior projects is a proven method of getting support from the community at large. And, for each community member who participates in such a manner, the personal reward of knowing that you have helped an adolescent to advance his or her education is very gratifying.

FINAL REFLECTIONS

With more than thirty years of experience redesigning high schools and providing professional development to schools and districts in the move toward a more student-driven learning environment, much has been learned.

Lesson 1. You can't change culture, or develop student agency, if you do not start with the students and understand what is possible. Ryan Marquis, a 2015 graduate of Pittsfield Middle High School in Pittsfield, New Hampshire, said in his address at graduation, "The student body will surprise you. They are smarter than you think and all you have to do is give them the keys. They might crash at first, but eventually they will learn to drive and they will impress you with where they end up." For students to be truly engaged and empowered, we have to provide them an opportunity to voice their needs and be fully engaged in the process to make major school decisions. This approach of developing students' agency impacts everything at the school, including their participation, leadership, and advocacy. It becomes the way schools think; it becomes the philosophy and pedagogy of the environment and stakeholders.

Lesson 2. Student agency takes on a different meaning, and can be implemented via a variety of best practices, based on a learning environment's unique needs. Schools may embrace the senior project, extended learning opportunities (ELOs), advisory, and site council and implement the purpose, structure, content, and assessment very differently than the school a town over.

How schools achieve success will be different, but the outcome will always be the same: increasing the level of student engagement, involvement, and empowerment to elevate the academic achievement of students and provide them with authentic learning opportunities to develop the skills required to handle the challenges and demands of the twenty-first century. The process is slow and deliberate work and may not be as tidy as we'd like, but it does mirror the cycle of educational growth and life. Student agency can be learned, but it is not easy. You need a strong vision, carefully constructed conditions, and the energy to act.

Lesson 3. People desire to be part of something larger than themselves—to have an impact and be part of an ecosystem of change. It begins in pockets and over time encompasses the entire learning community. It calls for a shift in thinking and behavior, but once teachers and students begin to see the impact of authentic agency, a school is able to make the full transformation to a student-driven environment.

Students want and need more say in their education. It is important to educate students for life in a democracy and help them see how they can help build their communities, in both the present and the future. The path to student agency will require commitment and time from everyone in your school.

You will find that enlisting students is a multiplier for progress in school redesign. Peggy Reynolds, former secondary curriculum director for the Nashua Public Schools in Nashua, New Hampshire, couldn't have said it any better: "If you've got students' interests at your core and all of your efforts are designed to move students forward, you are not going to go too far wrong. You may need to adjust your course a bit but if that's what's driving you, if that's what is pulling you forward, you are going to be okay."

Lesson 4. Our students are not stupid. It is up to all of us to create an educational ecosystem that releases the basic goodness and genius of each and every student.

About the Authors

Jason B. Midwood, director of innovation, strategic planning, and federal programs for the Central Falls School District, recently served as vice president of operations at the Center for Secondary School Redesign (CSSR). At CSSR, Jay was responsible for overseeing the day-to-day operations of the organization and supporting the growth and success of CSSR by ensuring that strategy and structure are aligned. He oversaw the development, planning, implementation, and follow-up for every project within the organization.

Jay is a leading voice in organizational change and student-centered learning and teaching strategies. He is an advocate for education redesign throughout Rhode Island and an advocate for student voice and choice initiatives in public education, and he sees students as part of the solution rather than part of the problem. In 2014, Jay was the recipient of the 40 Under 40 award by *Providence Business News*.

As project manager, Jay has gained a greater appreciation for the time it takes to effect school change. He has learned to embrace flexibility and ambiguity because one-size-fits-all reform does not work in the classroom or in the change process—you have to be able to adjust along the way.

Jay holds a BA from Rhode Island College, an executive degree in business management from Bryant University, and an MS in organizational leadership from Quinnipiac University. When not working to support schools, Jay enjoys spending time with his wife, daughter, and yellow lab.

Joseph DiMartino is founder and president of the Center for Secondary School Redesign (CSSR). Under his leadership, CSSR has become recognized as a leading provider of groundbreaking technical assistance to support both policy change and change leadership at the school and district level—leading to a richer, more personalized school experience for all youth.

Prior to founding CSSR, Joe served for nearly a decade as director of the Secondary School Redesign Program of the Education Alliance at Brown University. He oversaw the design, development, and implementation of numerous research and technical-assistance projects promoting high school redesign. Much of his work went into the development of the "breaking ranks" process of comprehensive high school reform, which has been implemented in more than forty schools across the country. In addition to his work at Brown, Joe has served as the chair of the steering committee of the National High School Alliance and cochair of the National Task Force on the High School, and he has also served on the Breaking Ranks Commission of the National Association of Secondary School Principals and the National Urban Task Force.

For Joe, the most enduring hope for his work is that students are able to take charge of their own learning. His experience has been personally and professionally gratifying, and has ratified long-held beliefs about the value of allowing for student agency as a vehicle for change.

Joe holds a BA from Brown University and an MEd in special education and counseling from Rhode Island College, and he has completed the coursework for a PhD in culturally responsive education from Brown University.

Joe is first and foremost a parent and grandparent, often stating that he has learned much more from his six children, including the four adopted from outside the United States, than he could ever hope to teach them. Helping to create learning environments where diversity is valued, as exemplified in his family, is his prime motivator.